GW00994412

SET FREE IN CHINA

SET FREE IN CHINA
Sojourns on the Edge

PETER HELLER

CHELSEA GREEN PUBLISHING COMPANY
POST MILLS, VERMONT

Permission Random House (Rainer Maria Rilke) and New Directions (Kenneth Rexroth—Chinese translation).

Special thanks to Jim Schley.

Library of Congress Cataloging-in-Publication Data
Heller, Peter 1959–
Set free in China: sojourns on the edge / Peter Heller.
p. cm.
ISBN 0-930031-53-9 (hardcover): $18.85
1. Heller, Peter, 1959– Journeys. 2. Adventure and adventurers.
I. Title.
G530.H394H45 1992   91-40238
910.4–dc20   CIP

To my family,
from Fulton Ferry
to First Place.
And to Lisa.

CONTENTS

LIVING IN A PICKUP   1

FRIENDS   17

LOGGING WITH HECTOR   34

THE MERCENARY   51

SEA WALLS   72

THE RIGHTS OF LOBSTER   81

JAGUAR HUNTER   102

A CONFLUENCE OF STYLES IN THE HIGH PAMIRS   117

SET FREE IN CHINA   136

CAPFULL CREEK   160

One cricket. The roads
lose themselves among the pines.
For what have I grown old?

LIVING IN A PICKUP

When I was in college I came into a small inheritance and bought a pickup. I went to Wisconsin to get it, because I'd heard that Japanese trucks weren't selling very well out there, and that you could get a better deal. It was true. On a muggy, overcast morning in Madison I signed the papers on a blue Toyota four-by-four longbed with a sliding rear window and a powerful radio.

"Should I break it in?" I asked the dealer.

"Go as fast as you want." He winked. "Just vary it some so the engine doesn't get in a groove."

I pretended I knew what he meant, and after he shook my hand I drove south around the big lake and east through a greening Indiana and Ohio and the warm May thunderstorms of central New York. I drove at fifty-five, sixty-three, seventy-five, and eighty- five going down long hills. I decided that the man had winked because going as fast as I wanted wasn't all that fast. Once in Ohio I drafted a Peterbilt semi and for four hours went a steady seventy with a light foot on the gas and two reflective naked ladies winking back at me from his mud flaps.

I slept once for about five hours. At a 76 Truck-stop I came to the fork with the sign for trucks pointing left, the one for cars to the right. What a choice. I turned left. I backed into a gap in the shuddering line of idling semis and fell asleep across the front seat. I woke up in a canyon of diesel fumes with a headache and a thirst for fresh air and never indulged that vanity again.

When I got back to New Hampshire I looked around for a camper top. I already knew that what I loved most in the world was to roll around the country. Between high school and college I had worked half a dozen jobs in half a dozen towns. I had worked in northern Vermont as a woodcutter, and in Rhode Island on a lobster boat. Later, in the summers away from school I had traveled to the Pacific Northwest and Alaska, where it was always easy to get work by the water. Now, with a truck, I thought I could rove from job to job and always have a place to live.

A friend sold me the fiberglass camper shell he'd had on his truck for $450, saying he was tired of not being able to see anything except forward. I bolted it on. It was plain white, a rectangular bottomless box which sat over the bed of the truck. It looked sleek to me. All of its edges were rounded. It had long sliding side windows with screens, a locking rear door— almost all window—which opened up from the tailgate, and a full-width skylight up front. He had bolted a two-by-four across the top and given me another which clamped to the roof of the cab so I could carry kayaks.

At the end of the spring I took a couple of trips with the camper, no modifications. Once a friend and I drove to Maine to paddle kayaks on the Kennebec and the West Branch of the Penobscot. Dirt logging roads go through that country for hundreds of miles, and the big log trucks take the corners at fifty and shake your front end and spray gravel as they thunder past the other way. When we paddled the Penobscot we could see Mount Katahdin off to the east presiding over all the wooded country. That was the trip an old-salt fly fisherman hailed us over at a broad bend and said in deep downeast,

"Hi theah. You fellas better set your brakes and have a look. There's a falls sets round that next bend."

We thanked him and he told us the fish were coy as schoolgirls, and then he squinted down his eyes and said,

"You're from New York City, ain't ya?"

My jaw dropped. I'd lived many years in Vermont and tried hard to acquire a slight upcountry twang.

"How'd you know?"

"I grew up in Queens," he said.

Our paddles and packs and boating gear rode beneath the camper shell, and at night I shoved them aside and lay my pad and bag on the ribbed steel of the truck bed and pulled down the rear door against the blackflies. I felt princely. I could see a couple of stars through the strip of skylight, and through the side windows the tops of firs bulked against the night. In the morning we went to a backwater convenience store above the dam and bought three-bite apple pies for breakfast.

That summer, my last term at school in New Hampshire, I went to the wood shop and bolted some two-by-eight legs onto a sheet of plywood, tall enough that they'd allow plastic milk crates to slip

4

underneath, and I had a proper bed. I lifted it into the back of the truck and put a piece of two-inch foam on top and a pile of blankets and an old down quilt. I was starting to feel that wherever I went I'd have a home. There was storage underneath, and about a foot and a half free along the left side to pile clothes, or set a cooler or wet gear. There were still a few kinks. When I took a hard corner the bed slid and knocked the sides. The milk crates were a great idea—I could fit about nine underneath, and still fit paddles along the side and a toolbox across the back. But once I pulled out the most rearward boxes, I couldn't reach the rest without bellying onto the tailgate and worming my way under the bed, feet peddling the air behind the truck. Once I did that on Main Street in Plymouth, New Hampshire, trying to find a snorkel and mask, and when I wriggled back out I found a knot of four little kids staring at me with funny half smiles on their faces.

I graduated in August and went to live with my Uncle George and Aunt Laura in Putney, Vermont. I thought they lived in the most beautiful place on God's Earth, a meadowed knoll overlooking the hills rolling down to the Connecticut River valley and the perfect gentle pinnacle of Mount Monadnock rising with the red sun over in New Hampshire. I loved these two, and had shared their hospitality often in the years I was at school in New England. I wanted to spend a little time there before I went out into the wide world. I unloaded my truck into their barn, took the cap off and slid out the wooden bed, then with the help of cousin Geordie lifted off the shell and hung it from ropes slung over old beams spattered with swallow shit. For a while I'd use the truck like a truck.

I read and wrote poetry in the morning, and did odd jobs in the afternoon to earn my keep. Mostly I cut wood. Sometimes after breakfast I'd sit with Laura and we'd drink coffee and talk about a book or the land for a while, or I'd read her one of my poems, which were mostly bad imitations of Frost or Wallace Stevens, depending on whom I'd been reading the day before.

Aunt Laura is one of the more calm, graceful, intelligent people I've ever known. She's a crack local historian and passionate amateur archaeologist, and I liked to listen to her accounts of the Indians who once lived up and down the valley, her theories of who the first European visitors might have been and when they came. About the poetry: I loved the idea of Robert Frost, a farmer-poet whose hands were calloused, who knew things. Knew which trees were which, how to prune an apple, mow a field, build a shed, kill a sheep, birth a calf. I didn't feel like I knew jack. Uncle George knew a lot. He'd built this house, raised the walls, laid the slate floor. Built the graceful dining table we ate on and drew the lyrical, fluid team of work horses in the picture frame there. He composed limericks while sorting eggs or stacking wood:

> The lamentable campaign of Hart
> was a screwed-up affair from the start.
> His detected erection
> deflected election
> when he traded the cake for a tart.

He could sail a boat, use an axe, distinguish fine brandies, and could be as witty as my own father, his brother, who is one of the brightest wits I've ever known.

One night while he was reading the paper and Laura was working on school board business at the table, I sat by the wood stove and made a list of things I absolutely knew. It was an odd compendium, including some of the following:

> "Do not go gentle into that good night" by Dylan Thomas and "Leda and the Swan" by Yeats. *archy and mehitabel. Roughing It.* "Anecdote of the Jar." "Asphodel" by Williams. *In Our Time.*
>
> Apples belong in Rosacea, flowers have five petals.
>
> White pines have five needles per fascicle, red two.
>
> Ponderosa bark smells like sweet vanilla.
>
> How to roll a kayak.

Conjugate *vouloir, respir, prendre*.

The dihedral of a vulture's wings vs. an eagle's.

What the Brooklyn piers look like in all weather, every season.

My family.

If the moon looks like a C it's waning (opposite of crescendo).

White wine with chicken.

There were a few cloying romantic entries like "the smell of Kim's hair," the rest of which I here omit. All told, it wasn't much. I felt pretty bad. I was just out of college and I couldn't even say with confidence, "My mind is a *tabula rasa*," because I had to look up the phrase just now to be sure what it meant. I could take neither knowledge of culture nor agriculture for granted; nor had the erudition I admired in my parents stuck to me. I knew that everybody inherited a certain knowledge by birthright, and I began to wonder what mine was, and what good it would do me. I thought of my truck. One thing I knew was how to drive it, and I loved to keep moving. That gave me some comfort. I could always hit the road. Movement is a great substitute for knowledge.

One afternoon Geordie and I were throwing heavy chunks of maple into the back of the truck which was backed up to a woodpile on a shady track that ran down to the brook and eventually up to the ridge behind Frost Pasture. Geordie had been just enough ahead of me in high school and college that I'd missed him at both. He too was included in the wide embrace of my admiration. He was—still is—an athlete, artist, and builder, and can be extremely witty, like his father and uncle. We were talking about great Louis L'Amour lines; Geordie had about sixty of the Western paperbacks on a shelf in his apartment.

"He was six foot two in his socks, if he ever had a pair." Grunt. Heave.

"I hadn't eaten in so long my belly was beginning to think my throat had been cut." Swing. Thud.

"I made a pot of coffee, strong enough to float a horseshoe, blacker than a canyon on a rainy night." Cradle, press, toss.

"You made that up!"

"Well, it should've been in there."

I got a maple chunk to my chest and lobbed it into the truck. It bounced, knocked hard against the single-walled steel and dented it from the inside. Well, I thought, got the first ding out of the way.

Geordie passed the back of a ripped deerskin glove across his brow and caught his breath. "You oughtta get a liner, Grubs. You're gonna dent that to hell."

I got one the next day. It was a tough, black plastic insert that fit snugly down into the inside of the truck bed. A concrete block would bounce and slide across it like a drop of water on hot Teflon. So would everything else, like a plywood bed and milk crates filled with everything I owned.

That autumn was one of the most beautiful I have ever seen, maybe because I had some real time to notice. But it's true that the colors of the turning leaves vary in intensity year to year, following dictates that not even old farmers can explain. In the evenings I ran down past where we'd dropped that maple, across the brook, and up a long deeply rutted track through mixed woods to the ridge and the pasture which was beginning to grow over with blackberry tangles and small pines. That year in late September everything turned gold. Not just the beeches. The oaks, a lot of the maples, birch. In the early evening, still warm enough to run shirtless, the sun came down through the canopies of yellow-gold and it was like running through warm honey. It was so beautiful it came in through my skin and I didn't know where to turn with the awe and love I felt. I broke out into the pasture and suddenly got the view of the folding hills and the orchards below and I wanted to hold all of it, to somehow make the country a part of me. Sometimes I flushed a grouse, and the sudden explosion of wings would make me leap. I guess I did take in that land, in a sense, because eight years later I am thinking about it and can just about smell those afternoons.

When winter came I parked the truck down past the barn and left New England, and didn't come back again for almost a year. When I did return I had one idea: I was going to outfit the truck and drift, picking up odd jobs as I went.

That August Aunt Laura sat down and showed me how to use a sewing machine. One afternoon I cut up a bunch of solid blue cloth and sewed some curtains for the camper cap, with velcro fasteners and nylon webbing to tie them back. For a curtain rod I strung a taut line between bolts drilled just above the windows.

I found some scrap plywood and cut it to fit tightly down onto the floor of the truck bed, above the plastic liner. Onto that I tacked blocks to hold the wooden bed from sliding.

There was still the problem of retrieving milk crates from under the bed. I bought a stout push-broom handle and screwed a hook into one end, and lay that in the back with the kayak paddles.

I put my favorite books in two of the crates, papers and files in a third, and clothes and gear and food in the other six. I had a small camping stove for cooking on the tailgate and a Coleman lantern, whose mantle was always crumbling, which hung from the upswung door of the shell. I made a foam storage sheath for the lantern so the mantle wouldn't break. From the curtain bolts I slung a light nylon hammock for storing clothes.

Along the side of the bed I snugged a cooler and a manual typewriter. My old .30-30 went in its cloth case further up the side, and at the head of the bed, beside the pillows, level with the small sliding window into the cab and front seat, I put a camera bag with a loaded .357. I knew I would be sleeping often just off the highway, and I had no way to securely lock the cap from the inside. Also, I grew up in New York City.

There's a Merle Haggard song I love. My old paddling friend Moby pulled out his guitar and sang it to me whenever I could persuade him. It's called "Rambling Fever." One of the verses begins:

I caught this rambling fever long ago,
When I first heard a lonesome whistle blow . . .

As a teenager, sleeping in the hills near my cousins' house, I'd hear the longway moan of the Montrealer down by the river, coming through at 1:00 A.M., then blowing again way up by Saxton's River, and it would send me nearly out of my skin with longing for the road.

One of the best places I camped was in a nature preserve outside of Hanover, New Hampshire, down a four-wheel-drive track beside a stream called Mink Brook. Eighty-foot pines lay a thick bed of needles, like light buckskin, over the ground. At night I worked waiting tables and washing dishes at a pizza restaurant, then drove out Lebanon Street and paused just before turning down the track to make sure no one saw me. Then I'd flick off everything but the parking lights and jostle and bump down a steep rocky grade until the trail leveled out and I could hear pine needles crunching softly under the tires. When I turned off the truck the night went completely dark and silent, and then the close ticks of the cooling engine and the warm night felt like a fine mesh, interstices filling again with the brushings of the pines and small rustlings and a single cricket. After a while shapes would return again, dark trunks, a vague suggestion of the road curving ahead, a piece of sky held in the limbs of the trees.

I slept hard, with the windows open and the breeze coming through the cap, and once in a while risked hanging up the lantern and reading by its strong white light before I slept. In the morning I shaved by the side mirror, and sometimes bathed in the brook. I ate cereal and bananas sitting on the tailgate. Then I drove up to town for a cup of coffee.

Landis, the friend with whom I'd paddled in Maine, was finishing up his last term, and I often went to his kitchen and set the typewriter on the table and fell asleep.

Another good spot was in West Virginia. It was a wide place beside a field on a dirt road which ran through the woods and old farm country just south of Martinsburg. A movie crew was in town filming *Sweet Dreams* and I was writing a screenplay with the movie's assistant producer. I shared a room at the I-81 Leisure Inn with my collaborator, a close friend from high school, and in the evening I drove out to the shoot location and ate a big catered meal on the house. One cold night at a little bar where they were filming Ed Harris dancing with Jessica Lange and he asked her if she'd like to "bump uglies," I found myself sitting on the other side of a post from Sam Shepard. I idolized the man, not because he was a movie star, but because I thought he was the best playwright in America. I always joked about having a bumper sticker that read "I'd rather be—Sam Shepard." I cleared my throat—my heart was stuck halfway in it—and told him I thought *Tooth of Crime* was a great play.

"I had a rough time with that one," he told me. "It took six weeks to write."

"Gee," I said, "that's fast! How long did it take you to write *True West*?"

"I don't time 'em." He was irritated.

I scrambled. "The critics say," I stammered, "they say you're a great talent but that you don't have a lot of discipline, that you don't rewrite. Do you write drafts?"

"I don't write drafts," he said sneering, "I write *versions*."

When we finished our screenplay, that's what we called it: "The Bestman, First Version." No one ever ended up buying it, nor the second or third versions either.

Sometimes my friend had a date and needed the room to himself so I drove out and slept at that spot by the road. I told myself that I slept better there anyway. I liked to wake up and stretch, and blink into the sun and the white mist hanging over the woods and fields. I wasn't very smooth with girls. Weeks later I finally got a date. Well into the evening I asked her if she wanted to go camping in my truck. It was raining and she looked at me like I was crazy and my heart thumped with the proximity of rejection. Then she smiled and picked up her purse and said, "This'll be different."

Two springs later I rolled the truck into a creek in a twisting ravine in the North Carolina Smokies. I was working there as a river guide, and was heading down to the company restaurant for dinner, probably going too fast. So was the other car; we met on a tight curve and I had to choose between the creek or the front end of her black Camaro. I crawled through the passenger window into the shallow water and looked at my tires pawing the sky. I was okay, and felt an odd compassion for the truck. The tow truck came and they hitched a cable to the front axle and hauled it out. I drove it away. I patched the shell with fiberglass, and after the body work was done, the fresh paint made the truck look strangely new.

To me the truck will always symbolize departure. The stories that follow are about roaming and working. Except for the next chapter, "Friends," the travels in these stories occurred either before I had the truck, or after I began to work for magazines when the trips involved going overseas and the truck was left behind. But the truck meant a lot to me, and still does. Aside from a showy over-powered motorcycle which I'd be smart to sell, it's still my only vehicle. It's beginning to rust, and there's something in the front end that shakes a little on corners at forty-five. Aside from that, it runs well, and I still have my sweetest sleeps on the bed in back, pulled over on a back road in some well-loved country, with the sound of the night coming through the screens.

FRIENDS

My friend Landis is dependable in that he is never on time. If he's in a car, he makes a great show of exceeding the speed limit as he pulls in to park.

"I'm sorry," he says, trying to look guilty. "I'll buy you dinner."

"I don't want you to buy me dinner, I want to go skiing this afternoon, which is moot, since it's no longer this afternoon."

I learned to adapt by anticipating at least an hour wait, which worked until he began to anticipate my anticipation.

I met him freshman winter in the dining hall at college. I had already heard about him. He was in my class, and he was on the U.S. Ski Team, a jumper. Naturally I was disposed to dislike him. During my nineteenth year I was strenuously engaged in carving out an identity for myself, just as in my sixteenth, seventeenth, eighteenth, and twentieth, and probably every year since. He already had one, as glamorous as could be. His arm, during that lunch, was in a sling, broken while sailing off a huge jump. There was a girl sitting on either side of him. He was tall, pale, with pale blue eyes and a beak of a nose. He was famous, and I was cordial.

A year and a half later I began kayaking white water with a vengeance. Landis was one of the handful of students who was already expert. Of course. He was from Colorado, a magnificent place I had once driven through, and it seemed he'd spent much of his youth paddling glorious rivers beneath snow-capped peaks.

The April of our sophomore year I started following him down icy New England streams, and learned several things about Landis that swept away the barriers to our friendship. One, he was fallible. He made mistakes in rivers, he forgot his life jacket, he was late, he was having trouble with a class, he was insecure about his writing; he was human. Two, he was generous and courageous. I saw him dart out of an eddy, and drive his kayak into massive waves above a very nasty drop, to save a swimmer who was out of his boat and powerless in the strong current. When someone else forgot their helmet after a long drive to a river he loaned them his, and paddled the day without one, which is pretty dangerous. Three, he had a peculiar sense of humor and he liked poetry. Driving to a river one morning, surreptitiously, like a man with a Bible in Stalinist Russia, he pulled a copy of the poems of Rainer Maria Rilke out of his pack and read me one about a gazelle, that beautiful lyric:

. . . .

to see you: tensed, as if each leg were a gun
loaded with leaps, but not fired while your neck
holds your head still, listening: as when,

while swimming in some isolated place,
a girl hears leaves rustle, and turns to look:
the forest pool reflected in her face.

Landis's face is a little like an eagle's. When he was done reading, he stared at the page, mute, blinking his almost colorless lashes. It was as if he were trying to look through the surface to the watchworks beneath, as if he were wrestling with the strange beauty, trying to fathom how something so nonphysical could work such power. He also led me to the work of Gary Snyder, and Kazantzakis. I was supposed to be the literary one in this growing friendship. I could quote Yeats and Dylan Thomas, yet I began to suspect that I was a bore. Landis just went into the stacks and picked books off the shelves and hunkered down in a corner, and his grades suffered because his assignments were never in on time. I started a magazine with some literati friends. We wrote high-minded pieces with debts to masters. Landis submitted a poem about boxes; it was about traveling with too many boxes, which is what he did when he went to ski competitions in Europe. It jumped off the page.

Landis took forever to graduate because he took the winters off to ski, and often the summers too, to kayak, when he might have caught up. He couldn't bear to miss the green, snowmelt river floodtime of June in Colorado. When he finally finished school and drove home for the last time, I was a few weeks ahead of him. That was the August I had been camping in my truck near Hanover, working as a waiter and writing in his kitchen during the day. At the end of the month I had decided to drive to Los Angeles to write a screenplay, and headed west.

It was a whim to stop. Landis's parents lived in a cabin at a place called Tabernash, Colorado. Tabernash has an eighteen day growing season. It huddles at almost nine thousand feet on the banks of the upper Fraser River. Perennially snow-heaped mountains look over the sweeps of lodgepole pines, the linked meadows of wheat grass and sage, the ragged lines of purple stemmed willows that run up the creeks in the hanging valleys.

Landis's father Andy is a doctor. He runs the clinic down the road at the ski resort of Winter Park. I hadn't a clue where their house was so I stopped in at the clinic and asked for Dr. Arnold. I had heard all sorts of stories: He was in the Mountain and Cold Weather Training Command in the fifties, a peacetime sequel to the Tenth Mountain Division which included a lot of top skiers and climbers. The troops had a great time in the Rockies, without worrying about getting shot at the end of their training. They loved to drink too, and I'd heard one tale about an officer sauntering into the bar at the Broadmoor Hotel in Colorado Springs and banging a piton into the oak counter and clipping himself in, to hang there from his harness while he got blottoed. Andy was reputed now to disappear from the official slopes and ski the deep powder in the trees where nobody else had the nerve, and I'd heard he'd swap anything for a day's hunting or fishing.

The man who came out drying his hands was short, red-bearded, with a merry glint in his eye behind tortoise shell glasses. He was very glad to see me, and suggested that I run up to the house. I did, and stayed a couple of weeks.

Landis's mother Becky accounts for my friend's stature and paleness, his high cheekbones and strong nose. She's a towering handsome woman. She's a direct descendant of Rebecca Nurse, the witch hanged in *The Crucible*, and is her namesake. Becky is stubborn, does what she pleases, laughs easily, and I can imagine her hanging before she'd recant something important to her. Come to think of it, Andy is much the same way, which makes for a feisty marriage. Becky has a bunch of horses to which she is fiercely devoted. She trains them, rides them western and English, and she boards the horses of her neighbors. Crammed onto the edge of a hanging valley, just beyond the clump of ramshackle cabins that crouch by the railroad tracks, the Arnolds have a tiny ranch.

Those were good days. I rode with Becky, who always welcomed help exercising the horses. Andy gave me a cowboy hat he'd found on a trail. At dusk I sometimes took out a horse and pretended I was a cowboy. I sang "Little Joe the Wrangler." We climbed the ridge east of the house and I sat watching our breaths smoke until the rim of light behind Byers Peak gave way to stars. I cut up some of their firewood, and helped with chores. Andy was fascinated with gadgets. He loved to tinker, and I spent a lot of time standing by his workbench, fascinated with his fascination. He collected old guns, old ski bindings, old pliers, ancient air compressors, and rivet sets. He'd pull a metal wheel that looked like a spur out of a drawer and hold it up to the light from the window and his eyes would dance.

"Know what that is?"

"A pizza perforator?"

"That there is an antique leather punch. An old guy up in Craig gave me that, must be twenty years ago. I think I traded him a pair of shooting gloves."

"Good trade."

Sure enough, carefully engraved on one side of the wheel were the words "Arnold 1963."

One afternoon a beat-up Subaru loaded with jumping skis and kayaks pulled into the gate and a tall pale kid got out and looked around as if he wanted the horizon of mountains to settle and be still for a couple of beats, so he could be sure he was home.

Seeing him arrive then was a little like seeing your brother, without any of the sibling static. I dropped a Sears and Roebuck fencing tool, and ran out of the garage to meet him.

That winter Landis would try out for the Sarajevo Olympics. So now he was in training. For him that meant leapfrogging in big circles around the yard, and going for runs he barely tolerated, and staying up late at the Slope dancing and playing pool and drinking too much. That's what we did, except I skipped the leapfrogging. We also paddled on the Upper Colorado, through Gore Canyon. I was having a lot of fun and I figured L.A. could wait a while. The second week we decided to go elk hunting, which neither of us had ever done.

We set up cans against the hill and shot them along with some milk jugs filled with water. Andy brought out about every gun he owned, which was a considerable number—odd prewar calibers I'd never heard of and badly balanced pistols—and we shot all of them. Andy never, ever missed.

Landis is not easy around guns the way his father is. You can see when he picks one up that he doesn't love it. It has a life of its own and that's okay with him. He respects it, and asks, in some unspoken way, that it help him. It's the way I feel when I pick up a camera. His dad had given him a .30-06 with a scope, and I had a little iron-sighted .30-30. Hunting season was already under way, so we had to go to Denver to buy licenses. I couldn't afford a nonresident elk license so I bought one for small game. We figured we'd hunt together, and if we got a bull, which wasn't likely, we'd use the one tag.

We didn't even get up early. We tried. We'd been out late. I had a crush on a redhead who taught handicapped skiing and loved to dance. She leaned into me and told me I was special, but wouldn't go for a walk. It baffled and depressed me when I thought about it. Neither Landis nor I can shoot pool for beans. Landis holds the cue like it's a Sioux coup stick for a ceremony he doesn't understand. He's a champion ski jumper, but the rituals of nocturnal society were somewhat alien. He strode up to the very serious local who had been dominating the table and said, "Hey, me and my friend will play you for drinks." I rolled my eyes. We won.

Beneath a high snowy escarpment is a gradually climbing system of ridges and swales all covered in lodgepole and spruce and carved with small meadows that locals call the Elk Patch. Landis and I parked beside a fence and bellied under the wire. No snow yet, except on the peaks; the meadows were brown and crisp, and the woods littered with crunchy needles and popping twigs.

"What do you think?" I whispered.

Landis shrugged.

"You want to spread out about a hundred yards and walk slow?"

He nodded. "Let's circle this ridge. There's a park on the other side." He said it very seriously.

Sometimes you just have to act like you know what you're doing. We held our guns across our waists and walked. Our breaths fogged. The grass rushed and rustled and whispered against our legs, painfully loud. Landis held up a finger. I froze. He strolled over.

"Can you hear me?" he whispered.

"Not really."

"It seems loud as shit."

"Yeah."

"The noise probably rises straight up."

He shrugged and walked back. We moved again. Every nerve strained. I had never looked or listened so hard in my life, nor been so pained at my own commotion. That lasted five minutes. I held up my hand and walked to him and leaned toward his ear.

"Shouldn't we move upwind or something?"

"Definitely." We looked around. We had both seen *Nanook of the North.* At the same time, we each took off a glove and wet a finger and tested the air. Simultaneously we jerked our heads toward our right. "We'll go cross slope first," he said.

"Good idea," I said.

Hunting like this was very tiring. At midday we collapsed on the edge of a wide grassy opening. Landis inherited his dad's propensity to be prepared. Once skiing they had gotten lost, and spent a miserable night huddled by a fire in the snow. So now he pulled out a windshell, down parka, sharpening stone, and emergency fire paste before he got to the cheese and sausage. Today I'm the same way, and I guess I learned it from them. We leaned against our rucksacks and looked at the wall of woods and the high white mountain that made us wince with its brilliance.

Landis said, "New England's claustrophobic."

"You always say that."

"I always felt crowded in, like the woods and hills were leaning on me."

"That was your professors, not the hills."

He grinned. It was true, because he never got anything in on time. He handed me half a chocolate bar, and I told him how it must be a question of what you're used to—how when I was traveling I missed Vermont. Not exactly missed it, but found that to me the prettiest places were often the ones that reminded me most of a northern New England landscape.

He said, "Did you ever take a course from Doug Ryan?"

Doug Ryan was a young professor with whom we paddled a lot in the spring.

"Yeah, terrestrial ecology. He nixed my 'A.' I thought I did 'A' work."

"Me too. He was hard on kayakers. He expected more or something."

"Maybe because he paddled a canoe."

Landis made a face.

"Naw, I liked him a lot. He was a good teacher."

"Yeah, he was. Remember when he swam Freight Train with all that ice?"

"Uh-huh."

For a while we stretched out and rested and didn't say anything.

Not two hours after lunch we were slowly approaching an old logging road when we heard a knock in the woods to our right and both froze. We looked at each other. Landis mouthed, "I'll keep going. You circle in." I nodded and stepped toward the trees. I went painfully slowly, carefully weighting each foot, stepping around sticks, trying to send my ears past the dense lacing of trunks and limbs that limited my view. I went about fifty yards and saw a movement like smoke, three or four or five huge shapes, then heard a single snap and they were gone. My heart raced. Elk. Real elk. Take it easy, I thought, stay slow. I figured that they, like deer, might get spooked, but would settle after a bit and stop again. It was like walking on a wire. Every muscle wanted to run forward, to close the distance. I calmed my breathing, crouched a little and stepped. And saw her. Down through the trees, the profile of a cow elk. I froze and stared. In among the tangle of branches behind her I saw the pale long line of spike antlers and nothing else. Ever so slowly I raised the rifle, twisted my left arm through the sling and leveled the bead. Wait, I thought, Wait. Settle. Wait—and he stepped into view. I saw the head, the upcurved patch of neck, thinking, Wait! Hold! Steady, don't rush; let out a breath, steady, squeeze, and—*blam*! He dropped. Quicker almost than gravity could have pulled him. I ran, and as I ran I was yelling, "Landis! Landis!" The elk was on the ground, neck stretched, tongue hanging, one depthless black eye to the woods, to me maybe, his legs jerking. I couldn't bear the idea that he might not be dead, might be suffering. I shot him twice in the head and got a lot of grief later for ruining the tongue. I stood, nerves humming, heartbeat reverberating, and felt a powerful and simultaneous sense of triumph and sadness and anticlimax. I felt suddenly drained. Then I heard a shot down the hill and another.

"Landis!" I shouted. "I got one."

A second later the words echoed back through the trees: "I got one toooo!"

Oh shit. The implications sped through the trees and landed, thump, at my feet. One tag, two bulls. Worse to leave the extra animal dead to rot. I left my gun and sprinted down the hill.

His bull was lying at the far edge of the meadow. It was a beautiful big five point. Landis stood over it looking at once completely pleased, baffled, proud, and sheepish.

"You got one?" he said.

"Yeah, didn't you hear me yelling?"

"I heard a few shots and yells. I thought you wounded one, so I took the last big bull that came out of the trees."

I winced and looked at my friend.

"I got it running," he added.

I shook my head and smiled helplessly. We had made a big mistake and I was very happy.

That was a strange sensation. I was so proud of us, elated, and incredulous too at the bounty that had just made me a bona fide poacher.

I let out a long whistling breath. "We better gut them."

"Do you know how?"

"I think so. Can't be too tough." I took out my knife and set the point against the taut, shortly furred skin of the lower belly. I looked up. Landis didn't look too enthusiastic. "I'll run along the ridge to Uncle Bill's," he said. "He's got an extra tag. Todd got one last week."

"Wow, yeah, go." He took off. Long-strided, running in his boots back up the old track. I think to him blood was pain. Another's pain, even a dead elk's, was always hard for him to handle.

We butchered the spike ourselves, dried a lot of jerky, and drove up to the Green River, near Wyoming on the Utah border. It was the end of October. That may be the most beautiful river trip I have ever taken. The days were sharp and blue and clear, the sandstone walls of Lodore Canyon were lit from rose-salmon to hues of purple, the box elders brilliant yellow-gold and the cottonwoods flaming orange. We saw nary another soul, and drifted for hours, numb-fingered, with flocks of Canada geese who used the river as a floatway south. They didn't take off when the water tumbled into heavy rapids, but bobbed right through, paddling deftly around hydraulics and yammering quietly in the pools. One morning a bald eagle lifted out of the tamarisk and flew ahead of us for several miles; his wings seemed to span the canyon.

We packaged and flash-froze the rest of my elk, and I put it in a box in the back of my truck and took it with me for the year in L.A. I drove twenty-six hours straight, because I was afraid the elk might thaw. Landis made the '84 Olympic team and jumped at Sarajevo, placed as the second American on the seventy meter, and fell in love with a Czech slalom racer.

Later, before he got married to Ivana, I shared a house with him in Boulder. I started seeing one of his oldest friends, a woman who had been his lover on and off for years. He said it didn't bother him. He loved this hardy, generous newspaper editor with the blazing smile partly, I think, because she never seemed to mind his long absences, their ambiguous friendship. But I fell in love with her. I thought he took her for granted. He felt that in the daze of infatuation two of his closest friends were cutting him off; maybe we were. There were a lot of hard feelings, some mistakes on both sides, and our friendship ruptured.

We went hunting that fall for a week in the Flat Tops with Dr. Arnold and one of his friends, had one shouting argument, and mostly spent our days cruising the country separately. Then, for a couple of years, we weren't much more than polite.

We have begun to do things together again, especially in kayaks, in the early summer when the rivers are raging. I get up to Tabernash when I can, because there is still almost no place I'd rather eat a meal and chew the fat. Andy and Becky's hospitality never lagged, despite the distance that grew between myself and their son.

This fall, in the middle of a hectic schedule, he came over to the Western Slope from Boulder and stayed with me; we went hunting again, for four days. We were very careful with each other, and we appreciated the laughter.

We parked up at the base of Chair Mountain in the snow and loaded our guns and walked out along a contouring path. A little ways in we stopped and I looked at him. I said, "What do you want to do, split up, about a hundred yards?"

He nodded seriously, and pointed around the drainage. "Let's sweep around like that. I get the sense they're staying high."

"Good." I watched him move down the hill. I thought how much I love him. And how our conversation is never as easy as it once was.

LOGGING WITH HECTOR

Sometimes it's just a name that tips your life north or south. That's why it was such a good name: Hector *Verge*. "Need cutter with own saw. Call eves."

Hector lived in God's Country, which is Franklin, Orleans, and Essex counties, Vermont, hard against the Canadian border. The TV weathermen like to say, ". . . and the country's low outside of Alaska, with a temperature of minus twenty-five and a wind chill of minus seventy-three, was posted again at Fargo, North Dakota . . ." I don't think they ever called anyone on the southern tip of Lake Memphremagog, where the north wind howls across the ice from the Canadian fir forests and hits Newport like a breaking wave and shreds the frozen woodsmoke which sinks from the chimneys.

Hector was a logger. French Canadian by birth, woodcutter by descent.

I met him on a Monday night, close to Newport on the Derby road, in a dark restaurant called the Charioteer. It had Elizabethan stained glass stickers over the windows, and studded aluminum goblets shading the lights. Hector was a slight man, all lank and knotty muscle, wearing a red wool hat cocked to one side and stained with grease.

"You Pete?"

"Mr. Verge?"

"Let's siddown," he said. He spoke softly in tone, manner, everything but volume, which was a decibel too high. I realized later that this was because he never wore ear plugs when he used a saw. Hector had huge ears, and he was half deaf.

Once in the booth he said, "Hector Verge," and shook my hand. He looked at me for a second, with watery brown eyes.

"You from Brattleboro?"

I lied. I wanted to be from New York City about

as much as a mallard wants to be from Central Park, so I shook my head and said, "Nope. Putney. Eight miles north of there." That's where Uncle George and Aunt Laura lived, and where I'd just spent three years going to high school.

"Yah," he said.

Well, now we were both locals. I felt better. He ordered a beer so I ordered one too. When the waitress came back, Hector took the bottle and glass and never let either one touch the table until they were both almost empty. His hands shook when he poured—bony hands that, like his ears, looked too big for him. The shaking might have been from the constant vibration of a chain saw.

"You want to cut?"

"Yeah."

"You got a saw?"

"Yup." I'd recently bought it, a black and red Jonsered 66E, automatic oiler with a twenty-inch blade. It was the pride of my life.

"You done it before?"

"Yup."

Saying yup a lot is a safe bet in Vermont, unless of course you say nope. Both are an agreeable way of taking the Fifth.

"Start tomorrow?"

"Sure."

"*Bien*," he said. The French startled me. He hadn't said anything about pay yet. I drank my beer.

"You got a place to stay?"

I shook my head.

He drained the last foam from his glass and wiped his mouth with the back of his hand. "You like kids? You can stay with us a couple days." He took two crumpled bills from his pocket and put them on the table, started to slide out of the booth. "Follow me."

"Mr. Verge?"

"Hector. Yah?"

"How much are you paying?"

"Four cents a foot for the eight footers, two cents for the fours." And he was out of the booth and heading for the door.

"Oh," I said to a female torso carved into the dark table.

Hector lived in Derby in a two-story wooden apartment house arranged like a motel. He drove a blistered blue station wagon with a coat hanger antenna and a CB whip sticking off the roof. We pulled up to a dirty snowbank and he got a paper bag off the front seat and knocked on the middle door. The bolt clicked and a woman stood in the yellow light, pale, with straight jet hair that curled outward at the bottom. She had buck teeth and was holding a little girl. Her black eyes were shadowed with fatigue. She looked at Hector like she was trying to place his arrival on the right line of a crowded daybook, then she caught me standing behind him and her eyes went hard and bright and back to Hector, questioning.

"Sue, this is our new cutter, Pete. He's starting tomorrow. Just drove all the way up from Brattleboro."

She didn't say anything.

"I told him he could stay with us a couple days."

All three of us were still standing in the door, and that's when I wished I had a van with a mattress in the back. Then she did the strangest thing. She smiled at me. It was as if she'd just weighed everything in her mind and decided.

"You eat dinner yet, Pete?" she said.

"Not yet."

"Well, come in."

The small vestibule led right into a crowded kitchen. It was stuffy, warm, and smelled of cooking. On the red Formica table were the remains of hot dogs and canned corn. Hector slipped two quarts of Genesee out of the paper sack, and a gallon of orange juice. There was another small girl sitting in a plastic high chair. She had a pink ribbon in her hair, a pony tail, and she sucked her thumb and watched me with round black eyes.

"That's Cheryl and this is Yvette," Sue said. "They act real shy, but they ain't. Sit down."

"I don't want to intrude—"

She turned from the stove, wide-eyed, her front teeth covering her lower lip.

"You ain't," she said simply.

After dinner Sue pulled Hector into the little living room and there was some whispering. There was a porcelain Virgin Mary in there, just to the right of the TV set. I could see her from my place at the table. Above her was a velvet wall hanging of five deer poised, listening, in a leafless forest. They were listening to you. Because judging by the brown woods it was November, and you were hunting them. I felt a strong sense of order in that room: our lives somehow hung exactly between the Virgin and the deer.

When they came out Hector said, "Pete, you and me let's go into town a couple minutes. Need some eggs."

We passed a convenience store on the way down the hill, but I didn't say anything. An icy wind buffeted the windows. We went to a supermarket on the close side of town. Through the bare trees on the edge of the nearly empty parking lot I could see an expanse of dim white—the lake. Stars glittered, perfectly still above the gusting branches. I felt terribly lonely. Hector came out carrying half a dozen eggs.

In the kitchen the three of us—the girls had been put to bed—drank beer out of jelly-jar glasses. I had Yogi the Bear. Then they showed me to my room. It was small, off the living room, nearly filled up with a double bed and a bureau. I leaned my pack against the panel-veneered wall, read half a page of a Louis L'Amour novel called *Hondo*, and went to sleep in my long underwear.

Knocking woke me up at six-thirty. I didn't know where I was. I'd been dreaming about playing pickup hockey on a lighted night lake, New Hampshire somewhere: all ice and pooled light, dark trees, whirling speed. The door opened.

"Like your eggs scrambled or fried?"

"Anything," I said, not remembering who was asking.

The door closed. I looked around. No windows. The overhead light was on, my pack was against the wall, felt-lined boots by the bed. On the bureau was a picture of a pretty young woman in a shiny white dress holding a bouquet of flowers. A trim, close-cropped young man, rugged even in the suit, held her right arm. He was grinning, and there was a humorous gleam in his eye, like he was saying, "Look what I done now!"

We had toast and eggs, coffee. At seven fifteen there was a double toot outside the door. It was bitter, probably five degrees. Windless. A jeep steamed its exhaust. I got my saw and gas can and the little sack with the sharpening jig, files, wrench, and cans of bar and motor oil out of my car. Hector and I climbed in back and crouched on the wheel wells.

"Pete, this is Sullivan and this my brother Marshal." They craned around and nodded. Sullivan was a pudgy man with blotched cheeks wearing a New England Patriots ski hat; he was driving. Marshal had short gray hair under an orange hunting cap, a lean handsome face with a straight-across mouth, and watery blue eyes. He looked almost like he could have been Hector's father.

It was freezing in the back of the jeep. I hunched in my wool coat. From beside the wheel well Hector pulled a small camping stove, and steadying a match over the lurching burner, lit it. My gas can was two feet away. He clamped the stove between his boots and rubbed his ungloved hands over the flame, motioned that I should too.

We stopped at a service station at a T in the road, and Marshal went in. He was a big man, taller than Hector by a head. He walked stiffly. He wore green wool pants, snowmobile boots, a heavy canvas jacket. He came out with a paper sack, and in the sack was a gallon of beer, a quart for each of us. Not for later, for now, 7:30 A.M. We took a right at the T, east. It was all trees here, a dark wall of fir and pine, with the graveled ice road cutting through.

Last night at the kitchen table Hector told me that in Texas he'd topped ponderosas. Some of them were one-hundred-sixty-feet high. He'd climb up with heel gaffs and a strap and cut the tops off. As the top fell on its rope he'd cling to the sprung tip of the trunk which swung in wide arcs before quivering to rest.

"How wide did they sway?"

"Goddam wide, wide as the sky. Ten feet. Pretty wide."

That's how he got to drinking beer before work.

"Those ponderosas was godawful high. I used to drink a six just to steady down before I went up there."

One thing bonded the Verge brothers as sure as genes. It sat at the edge of a clearing made by a power line, on a rise of churned and frozen mud: squat yellow, flat steel blade polished by impact and gleaming dully in the cold sun—a D-6 Cat bulldozer with a stake-bed trailer hitched to the back. Bought with borrowed money, used, second- or thirdhand, stubborn, immortal, ornery in extreme cold, the backbone of Verge Brothers Logging.

It wouldn't start. Marshal cursed. Sullivan just started picking up pieces of wood, and the brothers soaked a pile of wood chips and old limbs with gasoline and lit a fire under the engine to warm up the oil. Hector told me that we'd be clearing everything we could see on the other side of the power line.

Clear-cut. I think it's a pretty word, the sound. It's not popular, but to a logger it sings because it means you never have to stop. Start a hole, drop the trees into it, then circle the edges, felling inward, widening the hole to a clearing and the clearing to a field. Drop, limb, buck, and onto the next nearest tree. These were all softwoods, balsam fir, some white pine, scattered hemlock, all straight single trunks, so you never had to worry about the weight of the limbs. Hardwoods are top heavy; trunks divide, big limbs branch off and head north or south, and an oak or maple or beech can be heavily weighted to one side. It wants to fall in that direction, and if you want it to go in any other you have to think a little. That's when you bang plastic wedges into your cut, push with long forked poles, pull with ropes, hinge the back cuts, and are careful as hell. With a stand of second growth fir you don't think, you just move and hum.

Hector gave me an eight-foot measuring stick cut from the top of a tree and notched halfway. We were cutting "cedar rail" for fencing. All the butt logs were to be cut to eight-foot lengths, down to diameters of five inches. Logs smaller than five inches across would be cut to four feet. I walked under the power line and into the trees, the snow only midcalf. There's a strange sober elation in knowing that all the tall shapes around you will fall before your blade. It made me feel quiet.

About two hundred yards in I stopped, knelt, and filled the saw with gas and bar oil; took off the insulated rubber gloves and checked the cutting teeth with the back of my thumbnail. The edges were clean and even, and each tooth snagged and dug into my nail. Then I looked around. The lightly crusted snow was unbroken in each direction, but for my tracks. It had a light glaze, here and there the old tracks of a squirrel running between trees. The snow softened the contours of the ground, dipping and rising over hummocks and small hollows in smooth curves, like the surface of a very quiet sea. Tree shadows laced over it, needles and limbs in an anarchy of crisscrossed patterns, slender trunks all straight, falling over the snow in the same direction. The early sun winked in their branches; a single chickadee flitted and squeaked. I heard muffled voices through the trees, and then the diesel hacking and drone of the bulldozer starting up.

I picked up the saw, walked a few paces further, set the trigger, pulled out the choke knob, and winged back the starter cord.

Felling trees is a lovely action. You lean on the last cut, rocking the saw side to side, the cut opening only just perceptibly as the tree leans, barely unhinging, your eyes always moving from the cut up the length of the trunk, body well off to one side in case it snaps and bucks. There is a point of powerful stillness, a critical balance as the barely leaning tree seems to pause, and then with gathered force relinquishes its life in the sky. Just then, before you yank out the saw and jump away, you can gauge the direction of fall, and if you want to swing it a little further to the left, you cut fast and final on the right side, freeing it, leaving a hinge on the left which pulls it over. In this way you can actually carve a tree's fall, guiding it to the ground in a curving arc. There is a shuddering of air, a rush and crash of limbs, and you stand in the murmuring stillness, saw idling, as full of life as you've ever been.

It's easiest for me to approach the tree on my right, if it's softwood and not too big. I'm right-handed, so right hand is on the trigger, left gripping the guide bar. That means you can make the first cut with the back of the saw blade, level, say a third of the way through; then flip the saw over, go a few inches higher, and come down to that cut at an angle, so you carve free a wedge. If the tree is straight, it will fall over this notch. Then, without having to step around, you just move the saw to the back of the tree, and make a cut towards the wedge, and holler if there's anyone nearby. There's a lot of nuance, some fudging when you're working too fast, and different techniques for bigger trees. Most of these, though, were six inches to a foot across, and forty to sixty feet high.

Once down, you run the saw up the sides, limbing, and cut the trunk to length.

I was doing that to my fifth tree when I heard a yell over the saw. I turned startled. Hector was grinning behind me, his coat already off, hat over one eyebrow, sweater flecked with wood chips. I hit the stop switch and picked out my earplugs.

"Goddam good cutter. Lemme show you something. Save your muscle." He took my saw, yanked it alive. Then he set it down on the trunk of the tree I'd just felled and slid it forward. By tipping the blade sideways, flat along the top of the log, he'd lop any limbs sticking up; dipping it to one side or the other he'd shave the sides. He ran up and down the trunk, stepped back and nicked free a few branches from the underside and the tree was limbed clean, in about half the time it would have taken me.

He winked, handed back the saw. "Ya don't get so tired." Then he tromped back the way he'd come.

It never got warmer than about ten degrees, so we went home for lunch. Sue made us ravioli and coffee. Cheryl and Yvette stared at me, and Cheryl started to push her lips around and make funny faces. Sue stirred the noodles, and sucked on her upper teeth with her bottom lip. She didn't take her eyes off the pot while she talked to Hector.

"Burton called, wants to know if he can come by with the clam on Thursday." The clam was a log truck with a loading claw.

"Christ, we ain't ready. He said the tenth."

"He says he's got orders to fill, and needs you out of the way early." When she said that, color rose in her cheeks.

"Yah." Hector rubbed his eyes.

"How was it, Pete?" she said.

Hector perked up. "He's a goddam good worker. Got a good start. Ain't that right, Pete?"

"Yeah, it was great." I didn't know why, but I wanted to get out of that kitchen and back to work as fast as I could. When I went to the bathroom I heard Sue pleading with Hector to get the brakes on the car fixed, they pull left and almost killed them all this morning on the way to the store, and to leave her twenty dollars so she could get drops for Yvette's ear.

We worked until dusk that afternoon. I got into a rhythm, started a little clearing and worked from tree to tree, counterclockwise. I went as fast as I could, swinging up for the next tree as I sheered the final four-foot log off the last. Occasionally I had to stop and pile some of the logs, consolidate, so I didn't bury them with later trees. Hector told me I'd done good, probably cut about fifty dollars worth. He said

I'd make more as I got faster. Marshal agreed: "God-dam good," he said; he stopped in for more beer on the way home.

That night I sat on the couch in the crowded living room and watched a TV movie with the Verges, all about call girls and drugs in South Florida. That's when Hector told me he used to work high rises in Dallas and New York when they were first married. He'd ride the I-beams as they were craned up into place, and scramble to the ends and bolt them down. Sue held Hector's arm and nodded.

"Good night, Pete," they said when the movie was over, and went into their room off the kitchen. I went into mine, and tried to read and fell asleep.

The next morning I was on the way to the bathroom, and the door to the room off the kitchen was ajar. I caught sight of a crib, a toddler's bed, and a mattress on the floor, blankets askew. I went into the bathroom stunned.

What an idiot! Did I think they had *two* rooms with double beds? That's what they'd been whispering about the first night: giving me their room. They'd moved in with their children and slept on the floor, never told me.

I didn't say anything. That evening I drove into Newport and got a bare two-room apartment on Main Street right above a pizza parlor, forty dollars a week, with jukebox coming through the floor for free.

I cut with Hector and Marshal two weeks. Marshal missed about every third day, and Sullivan bitched about the cold. Hector cut about twice as fast as I did, and let his saw idle so the chain was running all the time, even with the finger off the trigger. It was wickedly dangerous. They stacked the logs on the trailer and pulled them out to the road with the Cat. The mill truck came on Thursday and took a load. The next day Hector gave me two-hundred dollars in cash and said he was still figuring. Linda Ronstadt's "Blue Bayou" came through my floor again and again at night, the bass thumping the walls with the wind that poured off the lake. One afternoon Hector offered me a case of orange juice they got free through the food stamp program.

Then it got cold, really cold. I stuck cardboard over the radiator grill to help my car. The saws had trouble idling, and it took an hour to start the Cat. When the wood smoke and car exhaust hung like a blanket over the streets, level with the eaves, Hector called it quits.

"When will we start again?"

"Don' know," he said, wagging his head. "Sometime this can go for a month."

"Fuck."

He worked his mouth, rubbed the brim of his wool hat on his forehead.

"I can't pay you now."

I nodded.

"You leave me an address and I can send it to you. You're a goddam good worker."

"Thanks."

I left him an address and left town. I never heard from him again.

THE MERCENARY

Sitka, Alaska is a fishing town on the ocean side of Baranof Island, to the south and across the straits from Juneau. It was evening and raining when the small plane landed. I walked across a bridge to the street that fronts the harbor. On the wide dock the metal sheds of Sitka Sound Seafoods rose in the grey twilight. Beside them a network of low plank walkways ran between the rows of seiners and longliners. The fluorescent pink of the buoys tied to the deckhouses and rails were the only bright thing in the harbor. Just beyond the boats small islets dark with spruce lay on the water.

Fishing boats at rest: tackle, lines, buoys, all tied off and salt-scarred, nets heaped, hulls stained and calloused with layers of paint. The violence of the sea written on every surface deepened the sense of peace. Drizzle sifted the slick water and the boats nosed the docks, gesturing at the dusk with extended booms.

A few days before I had been at the Fairbanks University gym, getting my first scrub after a five week river trip, and I had heard there was work fishing down in the Southeast. I hitched to Anchorage the next day, got a ride with a roughneck in a Land Rover who had a loaded .44 magnum between us on the front seat.

"What's that for?" Dumb question.

He nearly smacked his lips. He looked at me like I had just bought my ride, wouldn't have to pay for gas or anything.

"Up here they call that the Bear Minimum."

"Oh."

For the next two hours he told me bear stories. First bear and gun stories, like how a .357 will bounce off a grizzly's skull and pretty much piss him off, and how his buddy unloaded an entire cylinder of .44s into a charging Kodiak, and how some back-country guides load twelve-gauge shells with stacked dimes . . . I'd heard every one. I even had a theory that most men move to Alaska to talk about bears and guns.

In Anchorage I booked a flight and flew to Sitka.

Natural splendor has a way of turning loneliness into a virtue. As I faced the harbor, it occurred to me that now I could feel very bad or very good. There wasn't a soul within several latitudes I could call a friend; I was wet and I didn't know where I was going to sleep; the woods were full of bears and I didn't have the Bear Minimum. My heart was even broken, recently enough to be relevant if I thought about it hard enough. On the other hand, I was healthy, warm in my own skin and old enough to go into the bar across the street. It even made me feel good to think that I could feel really bad if I wanted to.

I leaned the pack on the boardwalk outside and went into the bar. It was well lit and smoky, and the jukebox was playing Tina Turner. The long bar was crowded, as were the tables and the booths. Saturday night. Two fishermen at the bar, almost as young as myself, gave me the scoop on work. The boats were mostly sewed up, but that could change any time, so it'd be best to walk the docks every few days; *Bobby's Girl* needed a new cook because the last one, a college girl from Minnesota, refused to sleep with Bobby, and her boyfriend whom she'd failed to mention at the fifteen-second job interview worked on the dock stripping freezers and had threatened to kill him. The *Marjorie Ann*, a sixty-five-foot refrigeration boat, was heading south after tuna, all the way to Mexico, and needed a net man. She'd be gone all winter. The cannery across the street, Sitka Sound Seafoods, was always hiring because people were always leaving.

The next person I talked to swore through his crumb flecked beard that if I had a chain saw I could make a hundred dollars a day helping him fill a government contract to log one of the nearby islands. I told him I didn't have a chain saw, not with me, but he bought me a beer anyway.

I ended up at a table full of surveyors for the U.S. Geodesic Survey, whom I trusted implicitly because they wore green ranger shirts. They let me spend the night on the floor of their government house. The next morning I got up early and walked down the sleeping hill to the cannery. A Filipino named Pedro pointed me to the offices in the south shed. I was hired immediately and then filled out an application.

That first day, during a break for dinner, I walked up the hill to the Salvation Army shelter and got a place to stay. Salvation Army Lieutenant Lum, a small, light-boned, mild-mannered Hawaiian in a starched white shirt, led me from his house and across the narrow driveway to the shelter, a modern ranch house with a spacious, open cooking and living area. He showed me to the men's bunk room. It had two double-decker bunk beds and a window. On one was a roiled sheet and crumpled pillow; from beneath it jutted the corner of an old army pack. Hanging from the frame of the upper bunk was a small plastic globe radio. I walked down the hill and went back to work.

Two more boats came in after dinner, we worked until 1:00 A.M. In and out of the freezers. Pedro is my buddy. He doesn't call me Peter, he yells across the polished concrete floor, "Hey, My Name! Come over here!" Over in the refrigeration shed we were throwing frozen salmon over the chicken wire into the holding bin. The Filipinos hate the Japanese, still. Pedro and William bit the grenade pins out of the heads of the fish before they lobbed them, yelling "The Japs! The Japs are coming!" keeping a fast work pace with machine gun bursts and explosions, the baskets of fish emptying with the speed of passion. Pedro lives in Hawaii. He hates Hawaiians too. He told me that his friend hid behind a bush and killed a Hawaiian with a poison dart just for fun.

Exhausted, seeing-double tired, I walked the mile up the steep streets to the shelter, shed my rubber boots and waterproof. A man came out of the bunk room, a black man in white briefs. He was ox-thick, wide-shouldered, with muscles in slabs. Sway backed, the curve of his lower back followed the curve of his belly. He moved stiffly. His body was hatched with dark marks, scars, his head glossy, free of hair.

"Kabu Kamon. You ca' call me Butch." Sullen-eyed, he looked at me. "You in my house. I gotta be up early."

"Yeah, sure. I'm Peter."

Butch went back to the room. I took a shower. The bunk room was dark but the globe radio was going. I spread out my sleeping bag on the bunk across the narrow aisle and stretched out. In my right hand, under the pillow, was a spring-loaded tear gas gun. The radio yammered.

"Hey, Butch." Whispering. Now voicing: "Butch!"

"Huh?"

"Could you turn off the radio?"

"Ever since Nam, man, I can't sleep without a fuckin' radio."

"Could you turn it down?"

The man pushed himself up. The yammer died to a pulsing whine.

"Thanks."

As tired as I was, it took what seemed like a long time to sleep. I was waiting to hear Butch's snoring, and sensed instead that he was waiting too, waiting up like a parent waits for a teen-age kid; though the radio must have meant that whatever he was waiting for never came home. The next thing I heard was the buzz of the travel alarm and I was awake, not sure where I was, and smelling coffee.

"Kabu Kamon, that's my street name, means Coke Head."

"Street name?"

"I'm a soldier, man. I been in Nam. Been in China. Got all fucked up in Africa. In France I did fuckin' Strengthofelevenmen."

"What?"

"Strengthofeleven men."

"You're a mercenary?"

"French foot fighting. They called me Peppie La Sleu. I'm a Seventh-Day Adventist. I fought for the Seventh-Day Adventists in Zimbabwe. I come back here and bought this fucking house." Voice rising. "This was supposed to be a Seventh-Day Adventist House. We had a deal with the Salvation Army—they weren't s'posed to be north of Vancouver." Looks at me. "Pete, you want some beans?"

*There's a tattoo on the very top of his head,
greenish black, just a cross of swords. I don't care if
what he says is true or not.*

*"Wait a sec. The Seventh-Day Adventists hired
mercenaries in Africa?"*

*"Protectin' property, man. I'm tired of this shit.
They tellin' me this ain't my house. I wanna be
back in combat."*

He pushes the chair back from the table.

I walked down the hill to the cannery. A cloud-
less morning, the town still in shadow, my limbs still
half asleep.

I was five minutes late: nobody was lounging,
drinking company coffee outside on the dock. Inside
the metal doors Pedro greeted me.

"Hey, My Name! You look funny."

"Yeah? What're we doing."

"First freezer. I think you been drinking."

Not drinking, dreaming. I felt like I was in a
weird dream.

"Hey Pedro."

"What?"

"You got a family?"

He held up four gloved fingers, grinning.

I didn't even know why I asked it, but it made
me feel better.

That night I got up to the house about ten. Butch was lying on his bunk in his briefs in the half dark, the light out but the door open to the big room where he'd left the light on for me. The little radio was playing. His hands were tucked under his head, eyes looking at the mattress of the upper bunk. I took a shower. Right over the bathtub was a shellacked wood cutout of the head of Jesus and beneath it the words, "You shall do Right by me." I guess they put it there to keep the needy from grabbing their puds in the shower. I went to my bunk and stretched out in my bag.

"Yo, Pete."

"Hey. How's it going?"

No answer. He reached up and turned the radio down.

"Thanks."

Long silence.

"Hey, Butch, I was wondering something. You said you wanted to go back into combat. Don't you get scared?"

"Sure, I'm scared. Everybody scared. But I got spirituality and the Lord above. I'm saved."

"Hunh." I chewed that over. Religious belief, to someone who was never brought up with it, can be like a refrigerator. You understand that it works, but still, the fact that you can plug a wire into an outlet and get cold is completely mystifying.

"You mean you like combat?"

"Everybody understand each other out there. Not like here. Here you're an animal. One time I was walking down the road in Zimbabwe and here come one of the enemy. He's a white man. He come right up to me, put his finger on my chest, say, 'Kabu Kamon, this ain't your fight man.' And he walk away. Turn his back and walk away. I didn't shoot him. But he go back to his superior and his superior slap him and say 'You out here to kill the enemy!' so he come back down the road and I shot him and he shot me and it was cool. Everybody understand each other."

"Woh." I was a little awed. In Butch's voice there was almost yearning. True or not, he was speaking from his heart, which scared me.

"You got a family, Butch?"

Silence. Then quickly: "Wife and two girls. They was blown away in a shotgun murder in Missouri."

I went to sleep. My body was too tired to let my mind wander. The tear gas gun was under my pillow and the radio was playing rock 'n' roll.

Butch worked on a carpentry crew in town. He left a half hour before I did, and walked uphill whereas I walked down. He had two shirts, a few T-shirts, work boots, and a pair of scuffed loafers worn to where they cocked badly to the outside. Underneath his bunk was the pack and a set of battered camping pots. And there was the house. He told me that he was seeing a lawyer in town about that. I never got a clear idea of why he thought he owned the house—except that he said he bought it once.

The nights I got out of the cannery by dinnertime I was so exhausted I steered past the bar across Catlea Street and walked home. Usually I stopped at the docks before I turned up the hill, and just watched the boats for a few minutes. Often the streets and docks were wet with rain. Out of the freezers, in heavy sweater and oilskins, the August evenings felt hot. It was still light. I watched crew members slip the lines from pilings and jump aboard, and watched the small seiners lug away through the islets, the diesel becoming drone and then gone. I wanted nothing more than to be on one of those boats.

At the house, Butch would be cooking; he offered me rice and beans, or spaghetti, beer, and I was too tired to pretend I didn't want it. He asked me what I did.

"I go to school. College. I want to write books."

"Storybooks?"

"Yeah."

"Ho."

"Sometime I'd like to sit down and write down some stuff about your life. When I'm not so beat. You wouldn't have to give me real names or anything."

"I ca' give you real names. You ca' write a book about my life."

That's when he told me I was his friend. He said: "Pete, man, anybody ever cross your path, I got a guy fly outa Juneau, see? You give him $275 down and his asking price and he blow his ass away. He don't fuck around."

I blinked. I ran the words through another time. Butch had just offered me the services of a hit man. I was touched. I said, "Thanks."

Sometimes the light in your world starts to bend a little. It's not that things are way out of place, or a different color; it's like putting on a mask and going diving. You reach for a shell on the bottom, pearl white and as big as a teacup, and you swim with it to the surface and break into the bright air and the shell in your hand instantaneously shrinks to something mundane, say the size of an egg. Salvation Army Lieutenant Lum lived just across a narrow dirt driveway with his large Midwestern wife. I sensed that that was where the air was. Over in the government condos on the other side of the hill, where the surveyors lived, that was probably air. It wasn't here, or down at the cannery: this was snorkeling.

On the dock I worked with a couple of big boys, local football players just graduated from high school, a few drifters, and a brigade of Filipinos.

Here's what happened to a salmon who thought she was going home to die and ended up in the hold of *The Party Animal* or *The Osprey*. She came to the dock, dead from exposure and shock. She was sucked out of the hold and heaped into a hopper with a thousand cousins and slapped onto the moving belt of the slime line where tired kids in yellow raingear flicked and sliced, the repetitive intricate motions of a dozen knives and a pressure hose scooping out eggs, guts, blood, and turning her into a sanitary sandwich of two filets, hinged at the back, led by a head and followed by a tail, the big ones regal still, all the way to the metal trays, four-foot square, where they were laid in rows and stacked on rolling racks.

Then the packers—strippers, glazers and loaders—took the baton and ran, which is just what it was like, a relay race under the high corrugated roof. A pair of us rolled the racks to the heavy doors of the flash freezers. Pedro or William or Ellen, someone who knew what was going on, yelled which one to load, and we clucked open the door and shoved the rack into a narrow aisle of polar frost cloud, twenty below, fogging us blind, grunting now over the cold-sticky steel to the very back, one pushing and one pulling, then we slid the trays into the rows of shelves.

Stripping freezers was another story. It was war. At 10:45 A.M. I might have just had two cups of company coffee and a pile of company donuts and a yell would echo across the expanse of polished concrete:

"Hey, My Name! You and me!"

Go: I ran. The idea was to jump into the freezer and slam the trays of frozen fish off the shelves and into a big wire hopper as fast we could. Pedro was already on the hopper, running, dragging it to the third freezer. I caught him in time to shove it over the lintel, the extra speed sending him and the basket headlong into the arctic fog "Oweee! My Name!" down to the back where the little islander was already striking upwards with a gloved hand, a precise furious blow that caught the edge of a tray on the top shelf and knocked it loose of ice-stick, then he stretched, both hands heaving the tray out and down and *wannng*! into the waiting hopper, half the fish still stuck to the tray, Pedro slamming it violently side to side until it emptied then yelling "*Tray*!" and I pressed myself to the side as the metal slab cartwheeled across the freezer, caught the edge of the door and ricocheted out onto the concrete floor, woe to the deaf and stupid, his palm already punching at the next tray down.

He was on the left side of the aisle, I was on the right, we were jamming, it was a violent dance, the trays slamming each other as they collided on the growing pile of stonehard salmon, the warning yells overlapping as the trays whomped and clattered out the door. A passerby would see only the open door and a hellish moil of frost, and hear the terrible commotion inside the cloud, and every few seconds see an empty tray ejected out of it. Our fingers became numb in the rubber gloves. Finally one of us yelled "*Full!*", both grabbed the thousand-pound bin, four feet scrabbled for purchase against the weight, sledded it past the door and *whish* out onto the smooth slide of the polished floor, passing it off to a pair of Filipinos who ran it like a team of miniature oxen across the floor to the glazing well.

There, a hook was slung to each end, the button pushed, and a power winch hummed and chattered it off the ground; they swung it over the well and lowered it into a pool of Karo corn syrup and water, which instantly froze in a protective glaze over the fish. Then it depended. If there was a shipment going out, it was over to the center of the floor for sorting by weight into boxes. If not, it was forklifted to one of the cold sheds where we threw the fish over a mesh wall into fifteen-foot-high heaps and the Filipinos yelled their crazy hatred of the Japanese.

Every two hours the company gave us free coffee and donuts. The average work day was fourteen hours. Five sixty an hour plus time and a half; $95.20 a day.

I was rich as Croesus.

I got home about ten. The lights were on, but Butch wasn't in the kitchen. There was a can of beef stew open by the stove, though none of it was emptied into the pan on the burner. I shed the slicker and rubber boots and walked into the bunkroom. The radio wasn't playing and he wasn't on the bunk. Then I cleared the corner of the door. Butch was sitting on a small table against the wall. There was a case of Rainier beside him and empties on the floor. His face was wet. He was still wearing his work clothes and his sobs were almost soundless, rising unevenly and catching in his throat. He was looking at the floor, the crossed swords on the top of his head shining darkly.

"Hey. Hey, Butch, what's wrong?"

He looked up. His eyes were fierce. He looked down and cried.

"I fought in Nam, I was a Marine. I gave my life for this country and they can't treat me like a fucking dog!" Then he mumbled something about a deed, about the house, how they were taking it away. Oh, shit.

"I's going downtown, Pete. I's gonna buy a black powder replica and blow Lum's ass away."

I sat on my bed. I reached across and slipped a beer out of the box and drank half of it.

"You wanna eat some stew? You left some stew out there."

I calmed him down. We drank another beer each. I heated up the stew, and in a reversal of the usual roles, I dished it out for him and ate some too. Butch was wasted. He hung his head and shoveled in the food, lost in a world of thought I couldn't imagine. Then he got up and went to bed. I was beat. I did the three dishes and took a shower, then went in and lay down. Butch was lying on his stomach in his briefs, a massive black man on white sheets; his head on the pillow was turned toward me and his eyes were wide open, looking across the patch of tile floor. Then he spoke.

"I knows I's a alcoholic. I knows I's a drug addic'. And I kills people for pay. I'm a sex fiend. I like to punch that vagina, stay in there as long as I fucking can. I put a contract out on my people in Missouri. But I'm saved. I got spirituality and the Lord above and I'm saved. Pete, man I'm *saved*!"

"I know it Butch. We better get to sleep."

I lay awake for a long time, the prickles running over the back of my neck. "Put a contract out on my people in Missouri . . ." A while ago he'd told me that his family was blown away in a shotgun murder in Missouri. . . . I didn't allow myself to think about that for more than a moment, but that was long enough to chill. I felt for the tear gas gun under my pillow, and then I felt for it again.

For the next couple of days, when I saw Butch, he kept suggesting that we could move in together, share an apartment, that I could work on his carpentry crew. He was scaring me. *Put a contract out on my people in Missouri.* One night he told me again how he would kill Lieutenant Lum. I liked Butch. He was generous and fiercely loyal. And the third day I decided I was getting the hell out of there.

At lunch break I left my raingear in a pile in the shed and jogged up the hill to the house. It was a bright blue morning. I stripped my bed, stuffed the sleeping bag, gathered toothbrush and razor and a few other possessions and zipped them into my pack. I was opening the fridge to take a yogurt for lunch when Butch came in the screen door. He was wearing mirror aviator shades and sweating into his unbuttoned shirt.

"Pete!"

"Hey, Butch." My guts tightened. I looked at him. "I gotta tell you something."

"Huh."

"I'm moving out."

He stopped cold. He took off the shades and looked at me.

"What the fuck?"

"I think I've overstayed my welcome. I've been

here two weeks now, and I'm not paying rent or any-thing."

He looked panicked. His eyes went around the room, searching for a place to pin his feelings. Then angry: "Did Lum tell you that? He tell you you gotta leave?"

"No, no. He didn't say a word. I just think I over-stayed my welcome."

Butch didn't know where to turn. Almost yelling he cried: "This is *my* house! You ca' stay here as long as you fucking want! I gonna kill that piece of shit!"

Then he was gone, a startling swift motion, the screen door slamming.

The next thing I heard was a scream next door, Mrs. Lum, and dishes breaking. I ran outside and across the driveway, in through the back door. Mrs. Lum was sobbing in the kitchen. Lum, his glasses broken and his mouth bloody, was picking himself off the kitchen table which had been shoved over to the sink. Butch was already gone. I made sure they were all right and jumped back to the other house. As fast as I could I strapped sleeping bag to pack, re-membered the sneakers under my bunk, then, think-ing of Butch's face when I told him I was leaving, I stopped. I dug out a pen and a notebook and scrawled a note: "Leaving town. You were my friend. I hope everything works out. Peter"—and left it on his bed. Then I grabbed the pack and—didn't make it.

Two cops came through the door followed by a tall trim-bearded man in a sports jacket. I whirled towards them, blinked twice and lowered the heavy pack to the floor. The tall man, blue-eyed, studied me. "You live here?" he said.

"I was just leaving."

"I can see that. Can I talk to you for a minute?"

I swallowed. "Yeah, sure."

I followed him into the back room Lum sometimes used for an office, and we sat on either side of the wide oak desk that had dwarfed the little lieutenant and now seemed proportioned correctly. He shook my hand. It was the most ambivalent handshake I had ever given. "I'm Detective Kreeger," he said. He took out a notebook.

He started to speak and I interrupted. "Look, Detective, I can't tell you anything. He was my friend. All I can say is be careful."

"We know him." He said it with a contempt I didn't like at all. "He's been in and out of this town."

"Can I go?"

He looked at me. "Yeah," he said drily.

I left. I picked up the pack and went downhill as fast as I could. Lunch break was just ending. Two young guys, slimers who'd shown up in the past week, were finishing their coffee. Keith and Dave. I'd talked with them before. Something about what had just happened let me forget decorum. I walked straight to them. "You guys got a place I could crash for the night?"

"We got a trailer out at Khe Sanh. C'mon." That was Kay's Court. A lot of the workers rented out there.

"Thanks."

I climbed the steps to the office and told them sorry I was leaving and left a forwarding address for the last check. Then I stripped my last slew of freezers with Pedro. When I told him I was leaving he just looked at me and nodded and said "." He'd seen a lot in his life; not a lot surprised him.

"You want some gum?" he said.

"Okay."

"Let's load the first freezer?"

"Okay."

That night in the cramped trailer Dave, Keith, and I partied hard. We smoked and drank beer and Southern Comfort. They were from Shelton, Washington, on the Olympic Peninsula. They had stolen Keith's father's car and some money from his bureau and come north. I told them I needed work. They said the father was usually hiring. He built concrete sea walls. You should go to Shelton, they said, but don't tell him where you got the idea.

The next morning I flew to Seattle.

SEA WALLS

Shelton was not a prepossessing town. Maybe it has changed, but when I was there it was not the kind of place you'd go out of your way to look up. It's logging country. Big firs cover the hills and crowd down to the inlets, and the Simpson Timber mill that perched at the edge of the water dominated the half dozen streets like a feudal castle. The tides rose and fell and the mill ran day and night. Loggers and mill workers fought with Skykomish Indians. There was no movie theater, and on summer evenings high school kids cruised up and down Railroad Street and parked in the lot by the Safeway.

My first memory of Shelton is walking down a country road in the evening. Tar, no stripes, blue asters and tawny end-of-summer grass, vine tangles and mixed woods. Behind me the sky was brightening down over the ridges, and I could smell salt water. I remember thinking, here we go again, new town, new job, new boss.

I unfolded the scrap of paper I had in my pocket and read it again. There would be a meadow on my left running down to the water, a copse of trees, and then the house.

I turned down a gravel drive, through a trimmed lawn and past a bed of pink and purple impatiens, as bright and unapologetic as the pigments in a watercolor set. A low, neat, redwood house stood before a stone wall. Behind it was an inlet with its dark water, and the darker backdrop of firs on the farther shore. A pickup with a steel lumber rack was parked outside the garage.

I set down my pack, reached for the bell, changed my mind and knocked. Standing in front of Keith's father's door, I had a few moments to reconsider. Why was I here? I wondered if I could be detained and subpoenaed. I wondered why nothing more compelling than a scrap of paper and the assurances of a fugitive had brought me more than a thousand miles to this man's house.

The door swung open, and I thought how in that instant one can tell a lot about what a person expects from the world. Watching someone in the sudden fanning space of a doorway can be like watching a face in sleep. Mr. Desmond pulled the door wide as if he was expecting a crew of workmen to file in and tear up his carpets. In a flash his expression shifted to suspicion, and he stepped up into the opening and cocked his head a little to the side.

"Yeah?"

He was a short man, broad in the shoulders, compact and strong. His thinning brown hair was short, and he wore steel rimmed glasses on a sun-darkened face that had nothing extra in the way of features. He looked like a hockey coach.

"Mr. Desmond?"

He nodded, I thought, a little warily.

"I heard you build concrete sea walls, that you might hire a laborer for a few weeks."

He seemed more congenial. "Who told you that?"

"I met your son Keith. He said you build the best walls—"

His eyes flickered and set up hard. They were dark gray, the color of the water behind the house; or of curing cement.

"Where?"

"Where? You mea—

"Where was he? What town?" Level. No emotion.

He was looking straight at me now. I dropped my eyes. I felt like I might turn into a pillar of salt.

"He asked me not to mention it."

There was a long silence, which filled dramatically with crickets and birds.

"Did he tell you why?"

He was standing square in the door, chewing the inside of his cheek. The question, the tone of it, was very restrained. "Yes, in part."

"Which part?"

"That he stole your car and some money."

"That part."

That's all he said. He was abstracted, looking right through me to somewhere else, to his son I suppose. Abruptly his eyes refocused and he extended a hand. "Dave Desmond." He seemed sad then. He nodded at my sweatshirt.

"Do you go there?"

"Yup."

"That's a good school. I knew a bunch from Dartmouth when I skied biathlon for the army."

He was trying to shake off his son, like water off a dog.

Dave was a good boss. He was high-strung and single-minded, and worked at speed, as if every job was an athletic event. It didn't surprise me when he told me one afternoon that he had nearly made the Olympics. On another day he mentioned that he had once water-skied from Juneau to Sitka, a world record at the time. When he said Sitka I thought of Keith and stammered that Sitka was a long way from anywhere.

The crew consisted of his stepson Rod, a strong overweight kid with loose straggling hair who cursed his jeans for riding down and never wore a belt; Mike Coleman, tall and pleasant, almost as old as Dave, with loud red curly hair and a short beard, who used to run a contracting business in Michigan, recently divorced; Mark, our foreman, long-haired, reticent, who worked in distracted haste and hardly said a word. And me, signed up at five bucks an hour, cash; eager, good at digging and carrying things around, but ignorant when it came to building a wall.

That is all we had to do: build walls. Hold the banks of inlets from crumbling into the tides. Buttress houses from spilling down the steep steps to their docks. Build the steps themselves, neat increments of defiance against gravity, weather, the sea. We were there to hold things together, and it was an odd bunch to be doing it, because that was something each of us could barely do with our own lives.

That first morning, after I'd slept on Dave's lawn, we drove along the north shore through forests of Douglas fir and past the stuttering gaps in the trees where a house or field let through a view of the water. Our job was to build a wall against a fifteen-foot bluff backing a narrow beach. A framework form of steel rod, or rebar, had already been constructed. Now predrilled plywood had to be bolted onto the outside to hold the cement.

Stepson Rod and I carried the heavy four-by-eight sheets down a steep trail of loose sand, slid them mostly on edge. Sometimes we lost control, feet scrabbling and sliding on ball bearings of small pebbles, struggling to brake and stay upright, finally letting go so that the rectangle of plywood spun and fell with a loud flop onto the sand. Dave glanced up sharply, but checked whatever he wanted to say. I saw that, and was more careful about holding on.

But Rod let them loose often, and I thought he did it on purpose—w*hoops*!—to test his mother's husband. After the fifth careening sheet Dave hung the claw of his hammer over a length of rebar, and climbed halfway up the trail.

He craned his head back and looked up at Rod. Evenly, voice measured and clear, he said, "Those are valuable. I've told you that. If you can't handle carrying them, I'll send up Mike."

Rod's round face was red with exertion; gloved

hands on hips. He wiped one across his eyes to clear the sweat and stared at his boss, eyes opaque.

Dave: "Okay?"

Rod nodded slowly. When Dave turned around Rod flipped him the finger. "Sure," he whispered, and after that was good to his word and didn't let a sheet loose.

We talked a little, as we turned to climb back up the path, or pulling the sheets free from a stack by the truck.

"My mom's divorcing him. We moved out last March."

"Why?"

"Can't you tell?"

I couldn't.

"He's an asshole."

In the afternoon I worked with Mike Coleman, helping lift and pound plywood onto bolts, and screwing the sections down with big wing nuts. The sun was bright and warm. However hot it got, Mike always wore a long undershirt, cuffs pushed up on his forearms. He could stand on the beach and press a sheet full-length over his head, while I hung off the framework near the top and lined up the holes in the wood over their bolts and hammered the panel home. I liked being up that high, hanging like a kid on a jungle gym, looking down the beach and across the water, swinging the hammer and talking. Mike laughed a lot, quietly, nodding his bright red, curly head. He never hurried. When a sheet was all the way in place he'd glance at me and grin and say, "Let's nail it," which was a holdover from his carpentry days. He was dependable and competent and he didn't care if the wall got built or not, he was just glad to be out by the water, occupying his hands, and away from whatever mess he'd left in Michigan. Once when we were both perched at the top of the form he pointed at the water. It was a narrow inlet. We were close to the curve at the head of it, and aside from a handful of docks and the roof of a house on the opposite shore, it was edged by dark woods.

"See it?"

"What is it?"

"Seal. See, just the head."

A smooth round figure cut a quiet V-wake and disappeared.

"First one I've ever seen," he said.

The sun dropped to the points of firs, the form was finished, a bulwark of plywood ready for concrete; the beach was still, a line of small debris lifting out of the lowering tide. A few stiff-legged sandpipers scampered on the damp sand.

Dave drove me into town. On the way he said he was raising my pay to six bucks. He asked me what I was studying. I said literature. He nodded.

"I wanted Keith to go to college," he said, and turned his head to the water.

He helped me find a room in a brick apartment building for thirty dollars a week. Only one left, no tub or shower. It had a small kitchen with a rickety table, and a bedroom with a double bed, stained mattress, and about a foot and a half between its edge and the sliding door of the closet. Smelled of must and the lingering staleness of sweaty clothes left in a corner. It was on the third floor, off a dim T-shaped hall, across from the common bathtub.

I thanked Dave and he said he'd be by at seven in the morning to give me a ride to the site. He gave a last glance around the empty kitchen—bare bulb, patched walls, single shelf over the electric stove—tightened his mouth into a kind of a smile, and closed the door.

That moment is frighteningly close to the heart of things. The first minutes in a bare rented room in a strange town are too much the way life is when you strip away the chatter and distractions: alone, coming and going.

My boss missed his son. I missed someone, but I didn't know who.

I slumped into the wooden chair. My back ached. I was too tired to eat. I pulled out the slick nylon tent fly, covered the mattress and spread out my bag, washed up in the kitchen sink, and dropped like a bird into a cove of sleep.

THE RIGHTS OF LOBSTER

I was sitting on the Newport, Rhode Island, wharf on a fine September morning. The harbor was bustling. It smelled of salt, fish, diesel, frying food. Tourists milled among the shops and restaurants. On the pier, where the lobster boats were tied to each other three and four deep, the great Aquidneck Lobster Company shed spilled harbor water from the darkness of its bay doors. Fishermen's pickups pulled in and out, unloading plastic barrels of bait, stacks of traps. Most of the boats were fifty-five-footers, twenty feet of high bow and deckhouse, thirty-five feet of low open stern. Crews swarmed over the decks and houses, scrubbing paint, lashing down gear, patching bait bags, tying sash weights to the bases of fluttering high flyers, the tall flagged buoys which were every offshore boat's banner and guidon.

Just shy of ten, a yellow truck swung onto the dock, and a squat powerful man with a red beard and uncombed hair slid out. His paint-stained corduroys were too short for him, too tight for his fat thighs. He began to peer from side to side, blinking back the brightness; I thought, "That's my man."

He'd said eight-thirty. His name was Tom Carey. He was a lobsterman and he was hiring me. He caught my eye and the first thing he did after shaking my hand was offer me a powdered donut.

The thing about fishing is that you don't get paid until you catch something. Ten percent of the catch, gross, was the going rate for crew.

The first day we drove to Carey's house and I tied rope bridles onto a hundred traps in the backyard.

The second day I helped him put a rebuilt transmission into his truck.

The third day he said we'd be shoving off in the afternoon and we went to pick up bait, forty-pound bricks of frozen redfish remnants wrapped in brown paper which we stacked on the open stern. His boat was called *The Rights of Man*. It was a year and a half old, and looked thirty. Rusty, filthy, deckhouse windows cracked. He went to get some line and sash weights and I idled by the company shed and had this conversation with an older man in yellow rubber Helly Hansen overalls.

Me: "Hi. Nice day."

Old Five Teeth: "Running ten-foot seas off the shelf. Wind coming up tonight."

"You don't say."

"You fishing?"

"Yup. Going out with *The Rights of Man*. First trip."

He looked at me, quizzical. Then shook his head. "You mean Tom Scarey and The Rights of Lobster?"

I let the air out of my chest. "Is that what they call it?"

"If I was you I'd think twice. I don't know a fisherman in this harbor that would go out with that sonofabitch. He's a danger. Doctor's son. Don't know his asshole from a rock crab."

Hunh.

That afternoon Carey said we'd wait a day for the seas to calm. Meantime we needed to repair a mess of nylon bait bags.

I thought I was being strung along.

The fourth day it rained and he called and said he had other stuff to do, I could stay home. Same on the fifth.

The sixth day broke clear and warm, and I went down to the pier and sat in the sun and sewed up holes in a heap of bait bags. I didn't mind; I felt picturesque, like a man in a Winslow Homer painting. Meanwhile the whole wharf reeked of the rotting redfish on the back of Carey's boat. A cloud of seagulls squalled and screamed over the free buffet. It was embarrassing. I heard other fishermen cursing Tom Carey.

That afternoon he walked up with a handsome skinny kid, my age, in an army jacket, jeans, and cowboy boots and said, "Peter, this is Dennis. He'll be going out with us."

We shook hands.

"Sure does stink around here," he said with a nasal drawl.

Carey said, "You all load up the bait bags," and left.

Dennis and I looked at each other. The fish were nothing now but a rank ooze, heaped by the rail and spreading over the deck, spiked with spines and bones, floating with the white cores of eyeballs. We scooped up handfuls and watched them drip through the mesh.

Dennis had hitched north from Jersey. He said, "Know Springsteen? He did a concert at my high school."

A few minutes later he told me he was a gigolo, part-time.

"You mean girls?"

He shrugged.

"Guys *and* girls?"

"Hey, don't get me wrong, I'm straight as an Apache arrow." He leaned towards me, confiding in his slow drawl. "It's like you scratch my back and I scratch yours. How we get along in this world."

"Huh." I'd seen *Midnight Cowboy*.

He looked around the oozing deck. "This sucks."

Late that afternoon Carey came back with three shopping bags and told us to unload them into the galley below, we were going out that evening. We took them down the steep stairs into a musty dimness. It smelled down here too. There was a grimy stove, a cupboard, a sink with bits of old food, spaghetti and congealed fat. Beyond that, two double-decker bunks covered with pieces of stained foam. All over the walls were taped centerfolds from Hustler. We started unloading. First a bag of Milky Ways. That's nice, I thought, at least he's thinking of dessert. Then a bag of tootsie rolls, one of sourballs, another of Hershey kisses. In the bottom were two boxes of glazed coffee cake. The other bag had more candy and sixes of pop. The third was all root beer.

Provisions for three days at sea.

We looked at each other again.

"You ever been out on the ocean?" I said.

"No, you?"

I shook my head.

Eighty miles of open ocean south and east of Newport, on the edge of the continental shelf where the submarine canyons run deepest, the offshore boats drop strings of forty traps, each a mile long. The traps are like the ones you see on the walls of chowder houses and postcards of Maine: four-foot-long cages of slatted wood or wire, netted at the ends with funneled openings that gape invitingly and narrow toward the center of the box where the bait bag dangles its promise of redfish. Lobsters live very much in the moment. They are gregarious, but not methodical. Once inside the trap with a clutch of cousins, it's very difficult for them to see a good reason to search for the small ring that let them in.

The strings of traps are marked by high-flying buoys, bobbing bamboo wands topped with flags, one at either end of the line. Each boat has its colors; *The Newsboy*'s were red and green. *The Rights of Man*'s black and yellow. The high flyers also support a multifaceted aluminum radar reflector, which looks a little like the star you put atop a Christmas tree.

The ocean is a vast wilderness. A week after dropping a string and steaming nearly a hundred miles home, a boat returns, plowing back through an endless heaving of swells, into a fishing ground whose horizons quiver with the swaying forms of high flyers from a score of other boats; one crew member perched on top of the deckhouse clings to an antenna guy for balance, all hands squint into the chop and fracturing of sunlight—and the boat, directed by his yells, diesel blaring, rolls right up to a tattered flag and a cache of lobster a mile long and a mile deep.

It was a lovely warm evening when Carey started up *The Rights of Man*. Dennis and I tossed the lines and jumped aboard, and we lugged out of the harbor. I was going to sea. The solid conviction that Carey was an idiot hardly mattered. I'd waited a long time to go fishing. I hungered to get out, out of sight of land to where sky alone ringed the horizon. In a hemmed world, the ocean is still a frontier. I wanted to hunt it. For me there was something fantastic in pulling life, and a living, out of the inscrutable waves.

We passed fancy yachts at their moorings, white hulls and gold-scrolled names gleaming in the long sunlight, neat dinghies bobbing. I had been off the dock five minutes, and already I disdained all these sailors of leisure. I was going to work. They could drink martinis and study celestial navigation all they wanted.

Dennis and I stood at the rail. The engine's vibration throbbed up through the steel deck, through bones, right to teeth. A salt breeze blew back hair, eyelashes. Over on the shore, tiny windows glared back the last sun like signal lights.

Dennis was a puzzle. Going into the open ocean in an army jacket and smooth-soled cowboy boots, whistling Springsteen. He was one of the oddest people I'd ever met. He was a hard worker; he seemed quite comfortable in his own skin; he lived without plans and bartered freely, without qualms.

The boat moved into the wind and a long easy swell with a tail of crying gulls. Night moved on the water and the upper reaches of the sky. The horizons still glowed, dim enough that the lights of shore prickled minutely. In less than an hour they fell off into the dark. The engine blared baritone over a bass throb, and over that was the rhythmic wash of the bow dropping into the swells.

Carey grabbed my shoulder, pulled me into the cabin. "This is our course," he yelled pointing at the lighted compass. He reached back and swung the door shut, muffling the engine. "A hundred and twelve degrees. Try to hold it. I'm going to get some shut-eye. In two hours put Dennis on the wheel, same course. If something blips within two miles on the radar, here," he pointed to the second ring on the green luminescent screen, "wake me up." He stumbled below.

"Okay," I said to no one.

The cabin was dark. Nothing but the compass light and glow of the small radar screen, pulsing with each circular sweep of green light. And behind them numbers winking on the loran recievers. Through the open window by my elbow, a fine netting of stars.

"Where'd fatso go?" Voice in my ear.

"Sleep."

"That figures. Want a cigarette?"

I shook my head. He lit up, sat on a tall stool by the port windows. The two-way radio jumbled with static. Dennis blew smoke, tapped his foot on the bar of the stool, sang something soundless.

"You got a family?" I said.

"Everything."

"Sisters, brothers, mother, father?"

He nodded his head, in time to his tune, visible in the light of the compass.

"You just travel around?" I said.

"I'm a traveler."

"Me, too." Kind of. Not like this kid. When I moved around I took a lot with me. Memories, connections, boots, and coats.

He sat with me through my watch, went out once to piss from the stern. When he came back he put a hand on the wheel. "Hey, check it out! Off the stern, man. Like stars. I got it, one-twelve."

I shoved open the heavy metal door, stepped onto the open deck of the stern and into the full blast of the diesel and fresh plashing of the waves, the tops of which sprayed back in a stiffer wind. Stars blew over the entire sky, unimpeded, down to the very darkness of earth's true curve. I'd never seen it before, four directions without hill or tree or rock to mark the night against. Steadying against the roll, I moved back to the open stern which had no chain or rail across it, and held on to a metal pole. In the rising-behind wake, green phosphorescence glimmered. Like stars.

Later, when I was on *The Newsboy*, that was my favorite time, the night watches, everyone else asleep, cruising between sets with just the light of the compass, the crackling of the radio, stars. I'd never seen the moon rise and fall in so many moods: sometimes a red pyre on the sea, growing into the prow of a crescent lightship climbing out of the waves. I wondered, holding on to the wet stanchion, phosphorescence churning below, completely alone under the Milky Way, how many sailors were tipped into the night ocean trying to take a leak.

Dawn. Carey shook me awake, out of dreams, the side of my face pressed into the damp foam of one of the bottom bunks. Though engine vibration came up through the bunk, it was a lower drone, quieter, and I could feel the boat corkscrewing, rising and falling easily as the waves passed beneath; there was no pounding wash from the bow. We were idling somewhere.

I got into my raingear, tore off a piece of coffee cake, and opened a can of root beer on the way up. Carey was at the wheel, nosing the boat into a four-foot sea. Ahead, off to starboard, a huge orange sun hung just clear of the gray vastness, which was all a rolling, heaving motion. A constant wind, not hard, but steady, pressed out of the sun's quarter. Then I saw what he'd been heading for, a reeling high flyer topped with tattered flags. Black and yellow. Dennis was leaning over the waist-high rail, gesturing at the dawn with a hooked pole.

"Grab it!" Carey yelled back.

We did. Carey was more animated than I'd seen him. Leaving the wheel with the boat swinging broadside to the swell, he pulled on rubber overalls and a green rainjacket and hustled out to the outside wheel and engine controls mounted on the rear of the deckhouse, next to the winch arm which swung over the water on the starboard side.

"Pull it in! In! There. Stash the buoy there! You, jump up on the rail and run the line over that wheel."

When I did he reached up with his right hand, his left on the wheel, steadying the bow into the waves, and deftly ran the rope in an S around the two wheels of the winch which was also mounted on the cabin wall. Then he shoved the winch lever forward. The motor sang, a steady electric hum, caught the dripping rope, stretched it taut with a creak of protest, and began to reel it in.

"You!" he yelled; he kept calling me *you*. "Coil the line in this tub. No kinks or we lose the show." I coiled it. I stood by the rail and fed the stiff line into loops as it snaked off the lower wheel, and watched fathom after fathom of fuzzed rope drawing up out of the dark water which rose and fell and rolled under the boat: a mile of line, dropping straight down to an unimaginable darkness of crags and ravines and darting forms and black eels and a clambering clawed cash crop. First there was a blurred form, a shifting of light in the darkness beneath the surface, taking shape. My heart raced. It grew bigger, and the yellow rope bridle broke the surface. The winch dropped a scale as it slowed, and the trap breached into air, water pouring from the slats, swinging around the line on its six foot lead.

"Grab it! The bottom end! Swing it up onto the rail!" Heave. I pulled against the solid weight—the bottoms of these end pots were lined with concrete—and swung it up and in; Carey reversed the winch to let the top end down on the rail, and then throttled it into full speed to retrieve the next, reaching up to help the trap's lead line run clean around the wheels of the winch.

Finally, excited, I took a breath to look at the trap. The side slats were busted. Inside we could see three pale rock crabs and a baby lobster waving its claws around. Dennis and I looked at Carey.

"Open it!" he yelled. "Put in a new bait bag, throw the lobster back."

"What about the crabs?"

He shook his head like he was trying to clear it. "Throw them in that wood box. We'll sell them." We did what he said and he told us to stack the trap on end in the port forward corner of the deck. By now the next trap was out of the water.

"Speed it up!" he yelled.

I waited for the boat to rock back, and using the momentum swung the trap onto the rail. It was considerably lighter without the concrete. There was nothing in it. One big rock crab clung to the outside like he'd claimed this weird pile of sticks. I knocked him into the water with the back of my glove, I don't know why.

We didn't need Carey to tell us what to do. We popped open the door, I unwound the string of the old empty bait bag from its nail, Dennis wound in a new one, filled with brown paper, and half lifted, half slid it next to the other trap in the corner. He almost fell as the boat lurched on a wave. He was smart: I watched him check the main line and the leads to the traps to make sure they were lying flat and clear. As he moved the trap, I quickly coiled the growing pile of incoming line into the tub.

The next two traps were busted, occupied by a few crabs. Another had two mature lobsters. Most were empty. Carey was at the winch and the wheel, silent, his back to us. I could see his profile when he looked to back the trap down onto the rail: his cheeks above the beard were fired with anger, lips compressed.

The whole set was like that. Nine legal lobsters, sleek shells of deep speckled brown. I thought, you guys weren't trapped, you were in the wrong place at the wrong time. The last trap, the fortieth, had a load of concrete and a long dark eel, which Carey grabbed by the endless throat and dropped into a plastic bucket beside him. We pulled in the second high flyer, which was missing half its flag. Dennis and I dragged the trap back, laid it beside the open stern, and leaned the flag beside it. Carey didn't say a thing. The stern was stacked now with eight rows of traps, half of them broken. I felt a little sick. Carey cruised into the swells for a minute, then told Dennis to take the wheel and hold the course. He swung past me, eyes blazing. I watched him and will not forget: with a violent gesture, almost defiant, his eyes raised to the fleeced sky just catching the sun, he hurled the tall flag and its float into the sea. Then he wheeled, crouched, and straight-armed the weighted trap over the stern. And screamed: "You!"

I hustled back. He told me to lay each trap down by the stern's edge, one at a time, as the one before was pulled into the water. "You got a knife?"

"No."

"Huh." He was weirdly triumphant. "Watch the lines then. One loop around a hand or foot and you're going to the bottom with all of those."

Thanks, I thought. Thanks for telling me. He moved back to the wheel, throttled forward, and one after another, as I danced to keep up, the line snapped taut, and the next baited trap jerked across the wet steel and back into the waves. The waves, it seemed to me, were bigger.

Carey was in the deckhouse, squinting at a chart. He took the wheel, swung broadside to the sea so the boat rolled sickeningly, and gave the *The Rights of Man* full power.

Dennis and I stood by the rail; he turned his back, cupped his hands and lighted up. "Man," he said, tossing the match away, inhaling. "That boy's got an attitude." His army jacket and boots were soaking wet. He didn't seem to notice. The wind, anyway, was not cold. He smiled at me. "Hey, we can have crab salad." Then he leaned over the rail and threw up.

That's how it was. The next string and the next. We were on the edge of the shelf, not too far from Nantucket. The water was warmer here, the Gulf Stream, and once I saw a bright blue tropical fish in one of the traps.

It was a half hour at most between sets. The high flyers of other boats wavered at the edges of sight. We banded the claws and dropped maybe thirty lobsters into the watery hold. Thirty. Not enough to pay for diesel. Carey didn't speak now. Once, when two traps came up together, tangled, he roared through gritted teeth, no words, just a deep sound from his gut. I felt seasick, not bad, just a leaded weakness in the stomach. The wind was steady, mostly out of the east, and the clouds were congregating into an overcast. I thought it was funny that we hadn't seen any other boats.

After the fifth set, Carey swung the boat back towards the Dump.

The Dump was a popular lobster ground halfway back to Newport. It was popular because it was close in, and it's where garbage scows dropped their loads which washed down to the voracious schools of scavenging lobsters. It took us four hours to get there. The wind was stiffening, the swells growing noticeably bigger, maybe six, seven feet. I gagged over the side a few times, but never vomited. I ate

Milky Ways and drank root beer. Carey turned on the weather radio, and a droning voice announced a gale warning. He turned it off, didn't say anything. I didn't either. I glanced at the set of his face.

We got to the Dump at about five, sky dense with clouds, already evening dark. Somehow Carey found his buoy among all the others and we began hauling in the string. More lobster now, a miraculous fifteen or so. It was difficult trying to stay on our feet and move the traps around in an eight-foot sea. The wind skimmed the tops off the swells and blew them in our faces. The bow, edging forward just enough to hold steady into the waves, tore chunks of seawater out of each swell, and they washed back. Dennis looked like a dog in a downpour, hair matted, clothes soaked. He never complained. He turned his head and closed his eyes when a pile of spray came back, and then he went back to work.

When we'd finished the set, and I'd helped each hopeless trash-baited busted trap back into the sea, staying as far back from the lurching edge as I could, I yanked open the cabin door and braced against the chart table in front of Carey.

"We're going in now, right?" I said, catching my breath.

His round eyes, set in the round red face, weren't even angry. He slid them over to me, and like a bully who's just taken a smaller child's candy and tells him that he can't have it back, he said, "One more string at least," and looked back at the compass.

I stared at him.

"You heard the radio. They're talking about a gale. Don't you think we should call it a day?"

"Good call," Dennis sang. "This is radical."

The bastard shrugged, and watched the compass and radar.

Darkness was dropping rapidly on all sides, not like the other night which was clear and edged with fire, but altogether, in an even deepening of overcast and air, until it was all the color of the sea. The bow slashed into the waves, tipped, and rolled, quartering, across them. The wind, unheard above the engine, shook the windows.

He was watching a blip on the radar.

"Go out and see if that's our flag." I stared at him. "*Now*."

He'd nailed it, the bamboo sliding along our side. Black and yellow. Hating the motions that my body was making, hating Carey, I grabbed it and hauled it onto the deck.

The spotlights snapped on, lighting the deck and the water off starboard. Carey burst out of the cabin and began pulling with me, taking in enough slack to run through the winch, then he started it. The boat heaved up and down, not pounding now that it was only nosing the waves. The rope tightened and ran, shedding silver under the white quartz lights. And it rose to the surface: a whitish mass that looked at first like the back of a whale, ghastly in the light, riding limp and dead on the moving surface, its coils spreading, awash.

Carey had hooked onto an old abandoned string, his gear tangled with thousands of feet of fuzzed and gnarled sea-buried line. Over the wind and diesel I heard him shriek, a cry of pure frustration. Then he turned on us, teeth grinding.

"Get up on the bow!" he screamed. "Take this line as I let it out! Then pull that rope in and pile it! God, that stuff's worth twelve cents a foot!"

He was mad. The sea was twelve feet now if it was anything. The bow of a lobster boat is a small triangle of wet steel, unrailed, with a cleat in the middle and two guy wires on either side, running up to the antenna. Most skippers paint their bows with grit, for traction. Carey's was slick, cold metal. Dennis had on cowboy boots. In a sea like that, in the dark, a man overboard would be gone forever.

I don't know why we didn't refuse. I grabbed the edge of the deckhouse, swung up onto the twelve inches of tossing deck running around it, gripped the handrail at the top and edged around to the bow. Dennis was right behind me, holding Carey's line in his teeth.

The bow rose and fell. The whale of line was luminous in the spotlight. We crouched on our knees beside the guy cable, which seemed firm, each crooking an arm around it, and then we pulled on the line which ran to the tangle. It came in to us, slowly. Carey was keeping the bow into the waves, so we weren't lurching sideways. Shoulder to shoulder, with the next dip of the bow we scrambled our hands on the rope and took in as much as we could, until the bow reared up. We clung to the wire against the sudden weight, and then as the bow dropped again we tugged in a few more feet. That was it. It was too heavy. We strained, relinquishing the safety of the cable, using our full weights, one palm slamming and bracing on the deck for the next dip, and took in nothing.

Suddenly the boat was corkscrewing wildly, turned quarter to the swells, swinging back, and Ca-rey was on top of us yelling, shoving me to Dennis's side of the guy wire, grabbing the rope and pulling with a fury. Six hands were on it now, the three of us perched on the edge of the crazily tossing bow, no one at the wheel, the boat motoring slowly forward. An image flashed through my mind of all of us pitching over, the empty boat cruising like a ghost ship into the wind-shrieking night. The recklessness of it ran through me like a current of electricity.

"Pull! Damn you, pull!" He was wild.

My shoulder was against Carey's. He was on his knees, right at the edge, heedless of the guy wire, all his fury and concentration on the line in his hands which slowly reeled the tangle up the side of the bow. The boat pitched. I looked quickly at Dennis, could just see his face in reflected light. Sometimes four eyes meet and there is a stark naked recognition that shudders. I felt it and saw it, and it was murder. One small shove and Carey would be off the bow. There were two loran receivers on the boat, no messing with channels, both coordinates always displayed. Setting a course home would be a snap.

A moment is a hair-tuned tripwire. We step over them all the time. And then, in heat, or folly, we kick one. And our lives are different afterwards.

We pulled in the rope.

The three of us grappled and swore and pulled in that mass of line and stacked it over the cleat, twelve cents a foot.

JAGUAR HUNTER

His office was on a quiet street behind the hospital on Avenida Doce, the blackened bronze plaque etched with the name: Manuel Castillo, Dermatologista. The door was a floor to ceiling gate of wrought-iron bars. I pressed the plastic button, and heard an electric buzz sound back from the deep shadow of the hall, and then a *tap tap tap* on the tiles. Unsmiling but pretty, in tight black pants and red high heels, the secretary turned the heavy lock. She led us down the hall. She said in succinct Spanish that the doctor was engaged. She said we might wait.

My friend Lisa and I were in Costa Rica for the winter. Our plan was to bicycle the west coast, from Nicaragua south to Panama. We had rugged mountain bikes, a pair of panniers each, a light tent and some small binoculars. We needed a ride to the Nicaraguan border, and we had heard that the doctor had a ranch in the far north and might be willing to give us a lift on one of his supply trips.

We sat in the leather chairs while an overhead fan rustled a potted jungle plant in the corner. The secretary read a magazine and ignored us. A young man carrying a small purse buzzed in and went directly to the rooms in the back, and ten minutes later he left. Twenty more minutes passed. We practiced conjugating irregular verbs, and then a door down the hall opened and the doctor emerged.

He was a small man. His dark olive skin was smooth, his arms thin, hands soft and neatly manicured. He had perfect white teeth and dark rings under his eyes.

"*Buenas*," he said and shook my hand. He nodded formally at Lisa, stretched his mouth into a quick, mirthless smile.

"Come, please," he said in English, and led us

back to his office. "Sit down." He closed the door, sat back in the leather chair behind the desk.

His office was almost a closet. We were crowded by a file cabinet and the photographs, mostly black and white, that hung on the walls. These were nearly all of great dead cats. Cats the size of men, dappled with spots, hamstrung and hanging from spreader bars suspended impossibly high. Cats stretched, heads to the ground, to fullest length.

Next to each of the jaguars, Manuel Castillo, dermatologist, stood with a gun. In half of them he wore a camouflaged helmet with headlamp that looked too big for his small, neat, dark head. He looked in the pictures like a little boy playing army. The smile which tightened his mouth was belied by proud, joyless eyes.

"My trophies," he said. He looked at me and raised his eyebrows a fraction of an inch. "Perhaps you are against hunting."

"No," I said. "Not in itself. But jaguars—"

"Yes," he said. "It is very sad."

He told us he had been the official jaguar hunter of Costa Rica, recruited by the government to destroy problem cats. He held the record outside of Brazil for the largest cat killed in the New World. He said that if he didn't shoot them, the farmers would put out poison meat and the jaguar would die a slow and terrible death. "I am a conservationist," he said.

He leaned back in the chair and steepled his small hands at his lips. "Alvaro Fernando gave you my name?"

"Yes, I'm a professional river guide. He suggested that we talk with you. "

"I see." His eyes were coffee brown. They looked steadily at us, rarely blinking. In his eyes was a light of interest, but no warmth.

"What is it you want?" he said. "You wish to visit the ranch?"

"We plan to mountain bike along the entire west coast, north to south. Alvaro said your ranch is just north of Santa Rosa, and that it would be a perfect starting point."

"Yes," he said. He blinked and smiled. The smile was perfunctory, almost as if he had remembered, in passing, a private joke. He leaned forward and pulled open a drawer. "We are starting an ecotourist company, with a lodge, offering tours of the dry forest and coast on horses. We have been talking to Alvaro about the possibility of sea kayaking. Here," he handed me a paper, "this is our brochure."

I opened it. Ecotours. Unique ecosystem. Tapirs, monkeys, crocodiles. *Jaguars.* Your vastly experienced guide.

"I am going there this weekend. I can offer you a visit. You are a professional guide, perhaps you can make us some recommendations. There will be no charge for the trip."

"Thank you," I said.

We left. Out in the hot street Lisa frowned. "Do you realize," she said, "that he didn't address a single word to me?"

"The only thing I care about more than conservation . . . ," said Manuel. He was speeding along the Pan American Highway, passing trucks and buses on steep curves, lunging up the spine of mountains that rose over the Gulf of Nicoya and the long spit of Puntarenas. "Fighting the Sandinistas, the life of the Contras."

In the back of the pickup were twelve new saddles, hammocks for the gallery of the lodge, and our bikes. On the floor beneath his seat was a holstered pistol.

"What is it?" I said, pointing. "A .357?"

He arched his eyebrows.

"Yes, do you know guns?"

"A little."

He smiled, genuinely. The truck flew up on the rear of a bus lumbering in a billow of black diesel. His eyes focused and his cheeks went hollow. Then he downshifted and hit the accelerator; the pickup jumped into the climbing curve, gained the side of the bus, and swung in just clear of the grille of an oncoming truck. I heard Lisa, in the little seat behind me, sigh.

"We have a training base on the ranch. We can start it up again in hours. We have a runway at Portrero Grande." He looked at me. "Big enough to land a B-52."

Portrero Grande was the name of a bay, and of the runway used in the infamous flights of the Iran-contra scandal, then less than six months old. Where we were going was no ordinary ranch.

We descended to the gulf, into a bright muggy heat, and the road straightened and shot into the arid country of the northwest. Manuel asked me to roll up my window, and he turned on the air conditioning. We flew over an iron bridge shaded by tall trees, the creek in the bottom running slowly with water. The dry season had begun, but in the mountains above, the cloud forests still caught the cirrus piling across from the Caribbean, and distilled them to rain. We passed woods and fields, blue concrete houses tangled with the vivid reds of bougainvillea. The country stretched itself out, flattening, giving way to wider plains of tall brown grass scattered with Brahma cattle, islanded with the umbrella canopies of guanacaste trees. To the east, dark jungled volcanoes were heaped with clouds, breaking on their ridge lines like waves. The black road shimmered with heat. Barbra Streisand warbled on the tape deck.

"Sometimes I stalk a cat for six months," he said.

He said that he waited night after night by the carcass of a cow; completely still beside his tree, measuring breaths. And one night he would hear the rustle of grass, the small hot sounds of the jaguar taking hold. His hand would go to the battery switch at his waist: a blare of headlight, the cat's eyes illuminated in surprise and rage: Explosion. Once he shot a cat through heart and lungs, and it rose and leapt and nearly killed him.

His face was impish, childlike, turned towards me for response. There was a light in his eyes that made me uncomfortable. It was as if he had just told me about ravishing a woman.

Liberia is the last bona fide town before reaching Nicaragua. It's a ranching town: Low stucco houses painted green and aqua-blue and pink, feed stores and dry goods, a lot of café restaurants and bars. There is a central plaza, filled with fig trees, and the unceasing ruckus of oropéndolas, and benches smattered with their droppings. In the middle is a gazebo where the police band plays on Saturday nights. *Vaqueros* from the nearby ranches, wiry dark men in straw cowboy hats, idle down the streets.

Manuel stopped in front of a windowless metal warehouse on the edge of town. "Come, please," he said.

I followed him through the heavy door. A man in a blue work uniform nodded at him. Stacked on every side were cases, in plastic flats, of bottled beer. Manuel turned to me. He seemed suddenly shy. "Which?" he said, motioning to a wall of bottles. "Which type of beer would you prefer?"

I pointed to the Pilsen, and Manuel insisted on buying three cases and paying for them himself. We carried the beer, and a heavy block of ice in a burlap sack filled with sawdust, to the back of his truck.

The gate beside the highway was padlocked. It was a caesura in a line of wire fence that ran off through the dried grass and scrub. Manuel set the parking brake, searched on a ring for the right key. When he found it he left the air-conditioned cab and walked into the blazing sun and unwound the wraps of heavy chain. I thought he looked out of place in that sprawling scrappy country: a compact neat man in tight designer jeans, engraved cowboy boots, and a pressed polo shirt.

The dusty drive cut west for a mile, through grass, groves of thorny acacia, guanacaste trees slick with heat. Muted greens and tans. We broke into a wide circle of beaten dirt and the surprising pulsations of bougainvillea that climbed the sides of a long, low, flat-roofed ranch house. A small cinder block shack sat on the southern edge, two half-dressed children playing in the dark doorway. Their mother, a large woman with dark hair to her waist, hung laundry—she glanced over and that was all. A young man in fatigue pants, muscle shirt, and camo cap ambled slowly past the truck carrying a machete. He nodded at the doctor and walked on looking at the ground. We got out of the truck. It was very quiet. I thought how the heat here must subdue people. A flock of parrots winged fast overhead, screeching, and disappeared.

Two cowboys, in wide bandito hats, emerged from the shadow of the gallery. They, at least, were grinning.

Manuel turned to us. "Maybe you would like to ride on horses?" he said. "Balantino will take you." He motioned to the thin man with the drooping moustache who seemed bent under the weight of his tremendous hat. Sure. The man smiled at us, bowed his head, and moved stiffly off toward the corral.

Costa Rica is so close to the equator that night comes at all times of year at about six. The sky above Manuel's ranch house was already a deep purple. We had returned from our dusty ride, full of the questions we would have liked to ask Balantino, who rode patiently ahead of us, threading the thorny trees, pointing to birds and once a large boa constrictor; but his Spanish blurred in a northern dialect we could not understand.

We sat on the edge of the gallery, drinking

sweating Pilsen beers. Nightjars sheared through the dusk with soft peeping cries. The cicadas were a low throb. A smell like chestnuts came out of the ground. The earth was shedding the heat of the day, would shed it in slow waves all night long.

Lisa relaxed at last in shorts and T-shirt. She is very fair and had spent the entire afternoon protected in long sleeve cotton shirt and long pants.

Manuel leaned back against a post. He told us that he had learned to love the land from hunting it. He said that between the house and the Pacific, twenty kilometers away at Portrero Grande, is a unique dry forest with jaguars, peccaries, deer, tapirs, three species of monkeys, and that he had hunted every foot of it.

"Do you still hunt?" asked Lisa.

Manuel smiled, quick and joyless.

"No more," he said. "We must preserve the jaguar."

"Huh." I knew her tone; it was an exhalation of pure irony which escaped Manuel. He looked at me, smiled again. It occurred to me that he was painfully shy.

"What do you think? Will the clients enjoy the riding? It is interesting country, *verdad?*"

"I'm sure they'll love it."

He nodded.

"You know," he said, "next year I plan to import zebras."

"Zebras?"

"Yes."

He was serious. The tall grass that is everywhere is jaragua, an African variety, perfectly suited to the zebra. With the herds, he said, there would be more food for the jaguar, and he could tranquilize the cats and bring them in from other parts of the country where they are being crowded out. Lisa flashed a look at me, tipped back her beer. To Manuel the world was a simple equation of predators and prey. What if the Contras attained complete victory? Manuel would have to import communists.

That night he took us for a walk over some of the same ground we had ridden. The light on his helmet swept over the huddled shapes of brush, pried into the branches of trees. He moved swiftly, and very quietly. Once he stopped suddenly, listened, and swung his light into the eyes of a big buck. I love watching someone suddenly in their element. A person can become abruptly graceful, larger than before. Manuel was completely at home in this darkness. We followed and said very little. He caught the fluid disappearance of a smaller cat called a jaguarundi. The reflecting pricks on the ground were the eyes of nightjars, ruffled into hollows. The eyes of owls glowed like taillights. Manuel was showing two gringos the country; but he was also hunting.

"This place makes me nervous."

"Me too."

"He's really being nice."

"Right."

"Let's start on our bikes on Sunday."

We whispered on the twin bed in the dark, newly painted room. A print of a jaguar in a tree looked down from somewhere on the wall.

The next day we went to the beach. It was at the end of a long, rocky road which branched toward the sea just south of the Nicaraguan border; a swath of desolate sand bordering a deep bay, surrounded by crumbled rock, cactus, and sparse trees. Manuel unpacked a folding plastic table with four built-in seats, a cooler with soda and beer. We helped him set them up in the shade of an almond tree. In a small canvas bag I noticed he also carried his gun.

He sat at the table in his jeans and boots.

"Why don't you swim?" he said. With each hour he was more talkative, more comfortable in the role of host. Now he was looking at me, his brown eyes rounded, familiar.

"Good idea. And you?"

"Perhaps later. There are sandwiches here when you are hungry."

We stripped to our bathing suits and jogged into the waves. They were too small to body surf, so we mostly floated. I felt Manuel's eyes in the shade of the tree. I waved once and saw his hand rising in the shadow. I felt edgy.

I paddled over to Lisa. "I'm not having much fun," I said.

"Me neither."

"We could start biking tomorrow."

"That's a great idea."

After breakfast I told Manuel that we were ready to begin biking south. He looked at me sharply.

"But you have seen nothing."

"We've seen a lot. It's beautiful. We have a long trip."

"Balantino will ride to Portrero Grande today to check on cattle and other things. He will be glad to take you, for two days."

It was a generous offer. We had never seen a guerrilla base or a covert airstrip.

"That sounds great," I said, "but we'd really like to get moving."

Manuel angered. His lips compressed, and his eyes darkened.

"I am returning to San José today," he said. "But I will come back on Wednesday. You can stay until then as my guests."

I didn't understand his anger or his insistence. It frightened me.

"You are generous," I said. "Extremely generous."

Two hours later, with barely a word, he dropped us off at the gate to Santa Rosa National Park, five miles to the south. We thanked him, but his face was dark, almost vengeful.

The rocky track descended, down and down through thick dry forest, twelve miles towards the sea. The bikes bumped and coasted. Flocks of parrots screeched overhead. Where the road bottomed out the hardpacked earth was deeply cracked, pocked with crab holes. A troupe of whiteface monkeys crashed in the canopy. Urine sprayed down. The trees thickened into denser mangrove.

Playa Naranjo was a desert of sand baked into the cusp of an elongated bay, scattered with the shells and reeking carcasses of great leatherback turtles. We pitched our tent just off the beach, under the trees. Waves crashed in. We stripped and dove into the froth, and swam out past the break. We bobbed there. A burnished sun touched the ocean and illuminated the green hills. A flock of parrots skimming the canopy caught the light.

The desolation was so great we barely spoke.

That night a poacher's fire winked down the beach. They came for turtles, deer, wild pigs. We lay in the tent, smothered with heat. All night long waves of hermit crabs chewed over the ground and scratched their claws against the walls of the tent.

A CONFLUENCE OF STYLES
IN THE HIGH PAMIRS

Yura Karpenko was not happy. He was squatting on his hams in the middle of a sandy valley in the Soviet High Pamirs. It was night. Twenty-thousand-foot peaks, sharp as shattered chips of shale and luminescent with snow, hemmed the drainage on all sides, so that Yura was crouching in a kind of roofless room. He was smoking a cigarette, oblivious to the campfire smoke that wreathed into his face, and the rising moon which moved south over the Afghan border.

Fifty yards to his right gleamed a shallow glacial river called the Balyandkiik. A mile downstream it joined a larger branch that soon became one of the most fearsome white-water runs in the Soviet Union— the Muksu, "Stormy River." One of the last teams to paddle it had lost five of their eleven men.

That was the river Yura thought he would be running; he thought he was coleading the joint Soviet–New Zealand Muksu Expedition, 1989. That would have been fine. But the Kiwis surrounding him wanted to go *up* the Balyandkiik, not down. They wanted to start paddling at an altitude higher than the highest point in New Zealand—12,349 feet on the summit of Mount Cook. They owed it to their sponsors.

Yura blinked. Maybe he thought he was in a weird dream. He sucked on the cigarette. Short, broad-shouldered, intense—I imagined he was strung together with piano wire. He shook his head, as if he were trying to clear it.

The Kiwis were insistent. The river above Camp One had never been paddled, and they wanted a chopper ride to the top, some twenty-five miles and three thousand vertical feet farther into the mountains. Though it was late September and the Pamir winter was not far off, they said they could do it in a couple of days and still have plenty of time to run the Muksu.

Vanya (translating, looking at his shoe): "Dmitry says you have no notes. He asks how can you make this river without notes."

Kiwi eyes flashed. It was a dumb question; what does anybody do who's running a river for the first time?

Kiwi (under his breath): "Notes? Mate, You're fucked in the head."

This trip, as much as anything, was a confluence of styles. The Soviets had done very few joint expeditions of this kind with anybody. In May the Soviet Peace Fund (originally established to help discredit and undermine NATO) had hosted a bizarre international raft race in Siberia; the New Zealand team, professional river guides who mostly grew up on sheep farms, did well. They outdrank almost everybody. They placed second behind Gorky, and as a prize for being the fastest foreign team were invited back to run the Muksu. They brought a couple of kayaks, three sleek self-baling state-of-the-art rafts, dry suits, and a crew of paddlers so experienced that one night at the fire I heard the same group of four talking about a rock in the Sunkosi river in Nepal, a certain wave on the Zambezi in Africa, and a waterfall move on New Zealand's Rangitikei. I was the sole American, invited as a kayaker and a journalist. I had covered the Siberia raft rally five months before for an outdoors magazine and come to know most of the Russians and the New Zealand team captain, Cam McLeay, on a subsequent expedition to a difficult river in the Caucasus.

The Soviets' approach to river running is completely homespun. They make their own gear. Their rafts are hand-sewn pontoons filled with anything that holds air and lashed together with stripped trees or metal tubing. A group from Moscow once filled their pontoons with hundreds of inflated condoms. And they often pay for river days with blood: so many pints donated to the local hospital gets an extra vacation day. Their big-water boats, called *plots*, look like floating oil-rig platforms. They are mammoth, maneuvered with two long sweep oars which jut from bow and stern, each worked by a pair of men who stand perched on a mesh deck. Just one of the three sausagelike pontoons holds more air than an entire Western raft. They are funky and ponderous, and the Soviets run rapids in them considered insane in the West.

So two traditions met. Like two streams of different colors coming together, they could run side by side for a long while without mixing.

Three kayakers went to paddle the Upper Balyandkiik—Mick Coyne, Roy Bailey, and myself. The chopper from Osh, returning with the expedition's last pile of gear, landed in camp, flattening tents, and we had five minutes to pack our boats and grab bags of food while Cam convinced the pilots to shuttle us upstream, higher into the mountains.

Three evenings later we drifted back into Camp One. The Soviets were relieved and impatient to get moving. Valera, a stocky, wide-faced railroad worker of limitless cheer, lifted each of us off the ground in a grateful bear hug. We had spent the days in a walled-in corridor of steep rapids too choked with rocks for anything but kayaks. On the second day we ran out of food. The last night we camped on a sandy bench covered with wolf tracks. I thought it was funny that the Russians didn't ask us any details about the river and never mentioned it again. I told Dmitry we did okay without notes.

"Oh," he said. "This river was made in 1975 with *plot* from forty-two hundred meters." I looked at him. At over thirteen thousand feet the Balyandkiik was weeds. The only thing that ran there might have been a marmot. Further down, where we had been, the only way a *plot* could get through was on edge.

"You mean, ours wasn't a first descent?"

He pulled at his sparse black beard and shook his head and wouldn't look at me. He was thin and stooped, with long unkempt hair and a tattered canvas windbreaker. He looked like a crazy scholar. Rewriting history. Maybe not. Maybe the Russians had come up here once with a tiny *plot* at high water and never told a soul.

I liked Yura a lot despite his unrelenting serious-ness. Maybe he was a little scared, like the rest of us. Maybe as Soviet captain and our host he felt ulti-mately responsible for everyone's safety. I liked him most when he drank cognac and grinned sheepishly and talked about Hemingway and the "Big Two-Hearted River."

Yura was a Moscow construction engineer by profession, responsible for building a section of the new American embassy. That was the one that was nearly abandoned because it is riddled with listening devices. I ribbed him about it. If I wanted to make him smile, I cupped my hand to my ear and whis-pered, "American embassy."

"I don't know about that. I am a normal man."

"That building's full of bugs. Someone put them in there. Right?"

"Maybe. I don't know." Case closed. I asked him if he wanted to set up my tent.

The morning after the Balyandkiik Yura helped me carry my kayak to the top of the main branch of the Muksu, about a mile over uneven moraine. There were snow leopard tracks running over the sand. They were everywhere up here. An upstream wind chilled the hands, and clouds, the first we'd seen, spumed off the peaks. From the twisting valleys, the mountains shot over ten thousand feet to their snowy summits. Steep flanks broke up into slabs and crumbled ledges, hued with bands of green, purple, rust. The cliffs seemed to be exfoliating.

The river came out of a hole in the ground. A hump of glacial milk, it shed itself on all sides and spilled into a raging gray rapid. A few hundred yards away the dirt-blackened walls of the Ferchinko Glacier calved themselves into pristine blocks of white ice jumbling in a shallow lake.

I was exhausted from three days of concentrated paddling on the Balyandkiik; I looked at the freezing river. Mick Coyne, a British expedition filmmaker, had the video camera out, and he was saying in his East London accent, "Now, Pete, pu' on yer life vest and ge' in the boat naturally."

I was afraid. Not of the water, but where it went: into a future of isolated canyons and weather and unimagined rapids, and out of a past where men had died. Roy and I squeezed into the kayaks and peeled out across the boil, and the current grabbed the boats and spilled us into the crashing, ash-colored waves.

Then the valley opened, the river smoothed and split into braids, and the team—three kayaks, three rafts, and a *plot*—was sucked into the strangest country I have ever seen.

Maybe it was the wind. From the moment we

put on, it stiffened. The river was a series of swollen ramps falling through a vast plain of small stones and sand, and the wind lifted the sand in blinding gusts which clouded the valley. The current tore along low vertical banks, offering no place to pull out. Loud clacks and chunks came from the water—rocks rolling beneath the kayak—and at the furthest edges the mountains fell in sheer, soaring rock slabs that were all grained like bark.

Around a swift corner the river split and split again, and I lost the boats behind me. Water was falling away in three directions, the wind howled and shuddered my lifted paddle—it was like being at sea. If the kayak turned sideways the gusts would knock it over. I sped by a rough projection of granite shore crowned by a gnarled juniper and a cairn of rocks and thought of the coast of Maine.

At a sharp bend, a creek spilled in from a side canyon, and I was on the Muksu proper, and there was nothing downstream but a walled valley completely obscured by the dark swirlings of storm.

Stormy River. Steinbeck said a man lives up to his given name: Edwin or Homer. Just ahead the Muksu was a blizzard.

I looked across the valley and saw the red helmets of six Soviets, just the tops, planing fast over the moraine. Their crimson flag, taut and bright, followed them like a bird. And I saw that the blizzard was blowing dust.

Sheer intensity, even amid immediate dangers, breeds a kind of ecstasy. It's probably chemical, endorphins and adrenaline, but I like to think it has a little to do with amazement. That night, in a niche clumped with willows, the storm cleared, cold stars breathed into a finely meshed blackness, and the Russians made a big fire in the shelter of a rock. They cooked their favorite meal: buckwheat and canned meat. They served all of us before themselves. Valera sat beside me and talked of his dream of taking two years to sail the Soviet Union's Northern Passage. He spent every weekend in a garage, helping friends build a thirty-six-foot sailboat. I asked him if he knew how to sail. He grinned and said, "A man can learn how to sail, eh Petrushkin?"

I was surprised again by the spirit of the Soviets. In the United States, if a neophyte wished to make an arduous sailing trip he would probably raise a pile of money, and buy a boat of proven design, and take instruction, and train for months, perhaps years, in local waters. Here they swapped for materials and built a boat and took off.

Mick Coyne was telling a story about basic training in the Royal Marines. Mick was thirty-one, six foot three, talked like a Cockney and looked like James Bond. He actually stunt-doubled for Roger Moore in *View to a Kill*. He organized and filmed wild expeditions that used combinations of kayaks and ultralight planes, rafts and skis, and got them into *National Geographic*. Then he would go back *National Geographic*. Then he would go back and do a similar trip with a group of blind and deaf, a man with palsy, and a woman with spina bifida. In the Royal Marine classroom, the sergeant had asked a question of a recruit on the far right side. A kid in the middle of the room answered. The sergeant was furious:

"Was I speaking to you? Am I *cross-eyed*?"

Mick, who was sitting on the far left, shouted, "No, sergeant!" The room leveled with laughter; Mick got himself beat up. He sipped his tea, winking, as we laughed.

Vanya translated as best he could. He was a young geologist who had learned his English from Frank Zappa records. He tried to explain Zappa songs to the Kiwis, talking excitedly about Stinkfoot and Fido the monster poodle. He'd say with animation, "Yeah, 'Pygmy Twilight,' I can't understand it all, really, to my shame," but in these larger meetings he was shy about his syntax and spoke in a near whisper.

The Russians smiled and nodded and raised their eyebrows, which was not to say they understood a word. They were impeccably polite. The Kiwis said stuff like, "Aw, g'donya ya bloody Pom!" ("Good for you, you damned Brit"), as Dmitry, whom the boys had started to call Dementry, manically pulled buckets of boiling water in and out of the fire with his bare hands and spilled half of them.

The next morning the river narrowed, steepened, bunched up like a horse ready to buck, and let fly.

Crouching out of the wind by a midday driftwood fire, Yura studied his notes. Rock slopes rose on all sides. They were so close that we could no longer see the tops of mountains. Yura said, "The next rapid is not difficult, but, well, rather emotional." *Emotional*. It was a wave train that looked like the North Sea in hurricane, dropping into a hole that swallowed the kayaks and spit them out yards downstream. Roy Bailey was a twenty-two-year-old Kiwi carpenter; he and I, because we were in kayaks that can usually rescue themselves, often ran first and set up throw lines in case anyone fell out of the rafts. Here's a conversation while scouting a rapid:

Me: "Man, that thing looks gnarly. What do you think about sneaking close to the wall and sprinting over the rock?" Subtext: "We're actually going *in* that mess?"

Roy: "Through the guts, mate."

"Oh, man, I dunno . . . "

Roy turned his almost sleepy blue eyes and looked at me with mild amusement. He had a diamond earring and packed-together wolf teeth. "She'll be right, mate." Then he walked to his boat.

I loved that—"She'll be right." There's a long lop-ing frontier optimism that walks out of that expression. It's like I imagine Americans used to feel about things.

With Roy, she always was right, and I started to have a lot of faith in this kid.

It was a bad day. We ran out of coffee. Brad McLeay, Cam's brother, was staring tuft-headed into the tin. His hair was so wild it looked like he was wearing a beaver hat. The day before the Russians had started rationing our sugar to four cubes per person per day. We began pulling out two tins of canned caramel each night and passing it around. Soon we ran out of that, too.

On the fourth day we hit the rapid "Etsell." It was rated Class VI C by the Russians, the top of their scale of difficulty and danger. It was a quarter mile long. Everybody walked down the bank and looked meticulously, picking out possible routes at every rock and hole and cascade. Cam, at twenty-six a merchant banker and possibly the best raft guide in New Zealand, was hopping all over the shore and saying, "Beauty! If you git a little low you can ride the pillow and take the right side, no worries. We can put someone with a rope here in case there's a swimmer. Hey, Ugly, look at that slot will ya?"

The Russians were more intense. They squatted in pairs and smoked and stared grimly at the water. I was getting the increasing sense that river running for them did not have a lot to do with fun; for them it was more like battle. I didn't envy them. I got the feeling that they were caught between a terror of the water—of making an error and being dumped—and a real fear of backing off and portaging a rapid.

It was an interesting contrast in machismo. The Kiwis were exuberant, wringing wry humor out of every exploit, and they were intrinsically farmhand tough. The Russians were deliberate, intent on conquering, and their courage was immense. Where we wore waterproof booties and dry suits designed to protect comfortably even while swimming in white water, they wore sneakers with wool socks and windbreakers, and Dmitry sported waderlike rubber pants that would pull a swimmer down. I saw Valera splash so often into the icy water in his canvas high tops to pull up the *plot*, saw Yura crouching against the wind in two layers less than I was wearing, that I wondered at the thickness of their skins.

Beyond these differences, we were all responsible for each others' lives in very direct ways. A Kiwi might be the one to throw a rope from shore to the *plot*, to catch it before it spilled out of control into the next rapid. Or a Russian might grab a raft and swing it up into the safety of an eddy. Everybody took their responsibility very seriously.

The rapid was unbridled wildness. Roy and I both got stopped and held, surfing, in a couple of spots before the hydraulics released us; the rafts bounced down; and the plot, levered side to side by the long sweep oars, ran with such finesse our jaws dropped. They steamrolled over the last ten-foot waterfall like a truck over a frog. When they pulled over they hugged each other in a big knot, and hooted, and banged the top of each other's helmets—and then everyone smoked another cigarette.

That night one of the Kiwis told me he had been passing Sergei's tent and was invited in. All the Russians were in there, and they were drinking coffee and eating a tin of caramel and one of ham. We hadn't see any food like that for days. Hoarding. I was dumbfounded.

Later I thought that it was probably just a private stash, and that maybe that was how they did things in the Soviet Union.

In books, when a vulture flies through the French doors, someone's going to have a bad day. We were in the middle of Fortambeck Canyon standing on a rock shelf, completely closed in by high walls. We were wet, and in the deep shadow it was cold.

That morning at a big meeting we had stood on a bluff above the river and Ura had talked at the ground. He had said to the Kiwis, "We adore your poise and skill. But now we approach the most dangerous section. We must not lose our concentration.

We must be aware of safety." Cam then proposed a running order, and suggested positions where he thought it was critical to station people ready to throw safety ropes in case of swimmers.

The rapid below us, called number 6, posed three problems. One, it was complicated and difficult. Two, at the bottom most of the river hit the lip of a ledge and slid into a deeply undercut canyon wall, which meant a kayak or a swimmer could get sucked beneath it, out of sight. Three, once you ran number 6 there was no way to climb out of the gorge—you were totally committed to running the next rapid, which we had only seen from high atop the rim of the canyon. Mistakes here could easily be fatal.

Roy, as usual, was telling me that we shouldn't have any problem breaking through the first curler and working right.

"Then what?"

"Then I'll see what happens."

Roy looked at me and suddenly his face changed. He pointed across the current. In a recirculating eddy floated a dead bird. It circled round and round. Its mate flew frantically back and forth, landing on a ledge, taking off again, searching, unable to recognize the lifeless carcass in the water. "Look at the bird," he pointed. "He lost his mate." Roy's voice was genuinely moved. "That fucking upsets me."

It upset me too, more, because I thought of Garcia Marquez: When the sky starts snowing rose petals, it's usually a sign. I had to make a deliberate effort to shake off my superstition. I looked again at the entrance curler, the way it folded beside a boulder, confirmed again that just off the rock a jet of current seemed to be pushing through; imagined once more what it would feel like to drive right, into the chop near the wall. Roy and I looked at each other and at the same time started walking to the boats.

I tried to get to the water first. I hustled my kayak across the tubes of a raft and climbed into it as if it were a race, stretched the spray skirt over the cockpit and said, "Okay!" and one of the Kiwis gave me a shove. I'm not sure why, but sometimes when I'm scared it's easier for me to lead off. I splashed into the current and took a few strong strokes to the far side, and drifted, letting the water carry me toward the first waves, and right then I made a small prayer. I focused on that curling spot in the approaching wall of white and broke into a driving sprint. Then everything was action and went silent. I thought, "Yes! Broke through, now right! Drive right!" I sailed through the complex rough currents beside the wall, surprised. A clear line was opening before me, without sound. I paddled hard and felt then as if I had wings, as if I were on a current that nothing could touch.

For me, runs like that in a kayak are rare, and

they are the times in paddling I cherish most. I splashed into the swirling pool below the final ledge and felt a current humming through my limbs. I guess you could call it joy.

At the bottom I was joined by Roy. We clasped hands. Relieved, we noticed the bird floating beside us. Then I thought *The bird came with us*; for some strange reason I found myself thanking the little pile of floating feathers.

Five days later the last of the Muksu's gorges ended with a big pool and a plank footbridge suspended between the walls. We were all alive. The pressure was lifted, and even the Russians were getting jocular.

Below, the valley opened and the river dropped more gently through wider views of desert ridges and mountains brilliant with snow. We decided to follow the bridge trail to what should be a village and buy a sheep. Kiwis know about sheep. In a yurt on the Chinese border the month before they had drunk *khumiz*—horse-milk beer—and gotten into an impassioned discussion with the Khirgiz herdsmen about range, breeds, and dogs. When our host had heard Dave Allardice could shear three hundred ewes in a day, he'd offered him his wife for the night.

The site of the village was an eerie place. On a rich green bench the walls of two dozen mud houses moldered into the grass. Sheep, a few horses, grazed.

Two large frame houses with tin roofs stood among the ruins. We walked to the first. An old Tadjik with a sparse white beard and leather Muslim cap met us. A frightened girl with dirty thin braids to her thighs crouched beside an outdoor dung fire. He ordered her to get us some crusts of bread and kefir. He didn't seem very happy to see us. We asked about a sheep. He shook his head. And his neighbor? We pointed to the other house on the hill.

"I don't know. I don't speak with him."

We walked to the next house. On a post outside was a red plastic rafter's helmet. Another old man welcomed us. In a dark room with one window he motioned for us to sit on the quilts along the wall and to share his wooden bowl of rice pudding, his pot of tea. Young women, heavily shawled, cracked the door to peer at us, and we could hear their giggles. This man told us a story.

In 1987, when a Soviet catamaran flipped on the river and drowned five men, one paddler was caught in the frame and pulled downstream. He floated for miles. In the calm at the footbridge he managed to get ashore. His leg was broken in two places and he was nearly dead from exposure. His clothes, but for his helmet and a couple of shreds, had been ripped off by the powerful currents. He crawled to the bridge and up the track. The wrong way. There was nothing on that bank but an old tomb and a cemetery of sunken graves. He crawled back, across the bridge.

It was night. Back along the trail we had just walked, two miles, until he saw the light of a house. The man knocked, moaned; a woman opened, saw him and began to yell. She slammed the door. He would not die there. He turned and got to the door of our host who seized him, lay him down by the stove, and for the next week as the rafter drifted in and out of coma, tended him. When the helicopters came, the man was stable.

So now our host would not talk to his neighbor. He said, "He takes, but he will not give." These two families were the only human inhabitants within miles, and they were not speaking to each other.

We bought a sheep, set her in the middle of a raft with a life jacket on (she chewed her cud through several rapids), and ate her that night at our last camp on the Muksu. Dima set off flares, Dmitry poured an entire box of tea into the bucket so that the Kiwis were spitting it in the sand and mumbling, "Fucking Dementry, who let 'im near the cooking?" and Valera poured out an inch of vodka in nineteen enamel cups. We toasted. Valera said something about victory over ourselves. Cam raised his cup.

"G'donya, boys. Get it down ya." He winked and drank.

Later that night, by the fire, I heard Vanya trying to explain the song "Penguins in Bondage" to Roy.

SET FREE IN CHINA

In the lobby of the Minshan Hotel in Chengdu, a string quartet rests their bows while a porcelain faced woman sings Italian opera. Outside the glass doors, a fountain blooms yellow and orange, and pours in a sheet off the portico. Beyond that lies the Avenue of the People: in a crush of bicycles and jangling bells, brightly clad workers peddle toward, and away from, a giant white statue of Mao.

I am here, strangely, to kayak white water.

Scott Heywood, an outfitter from Sheridan, Wyoming, stares out the window of our room on the eighteenth floor. A phalanx of Soviet-style apartment buildings stretches away into a permanent dusk of coal smoke. Beneath them, the low, black-tile roofs of old China make a chaotic patchwork. Alone on the dirt of a deserted schoolyard, a woman sways through the motions of tai chi, stops abruptly, and hits a button on her digital watch.

Scott sips jasmine tea from a thermos. "I can't believe we're here," he says. "I think I'm dreaming. Am I dreaming?"

At forty his eyes ask like a kid's. Short and compact, a high school wrestler turned mountaineer and paddler, Scott reminds me of Garp. He yanks at his cropped beard.

"Listen."

Through the wall we can still hear the arguing. A group of American climbers heading for the Chinese Pamirs is haggling with officials over camels. Government regulations prescribe one camel for every three people; the climbers insist they need more, and will pay. But it's not a matter of money. The regulation is there for anyone to read—anyone who can read Mandarin.

The tableaux unfolding all around me are so odd, I'm not certain I can reassure Scott. I feel a little like I'm dreaming too. Twelve of us have come here to make first descents of the Dadu River and its tributaries; all experienced paddlers except for Dave DuVal and his British bride, Fiona, who are here on their honeymoon. The trip has been painstakingly prepared by Kent Madin of Boojum Expeditions, San Diego. The expedition has been subsidized in part by the Chinese government, which is eager to promote adventure travel, even after Ken Warren's disastrous exploit on the Yangtze River three years ago when a team member died of altitude sickness. The Chinese have provided two drivers and four overland guides who will take care of logistics, translating, and cooking whenever we need to camp. It's a kayaker's fantasy. Gazing out the window, I think of the old Taoist sage, Chuang Tzu, who dreamt he was a butterfly, and woke up wondering if he were really a butterfly dreaming he was Chuang Tzu.

The Dadu River, a tributary of the Yangtze, flows south off the eastern edge of the Tibetan plateau in what is now western Sichuan province. It's a rugged, remote land of snowy, fourteen-thousand-foot passes, precipitous wooded canyons, and Buddhist villages belonging more to Tibet than to China, which has controlled them since the early fifties. The section we would run shares a canyon with a crumbling shale road, from which the river has been scouted and characterized as Class III with a little Class IV.

On September 19, Lao Win, samurai driver, blasted our Coaster bus west across the rice flats. A tiny man in black-leather gloves and a red fly-fishing hat pulled tight over his ears, he rarely let off the horn. If he did, it was only to hurl *Road-Warrior* epithets out the open window. Careening up switchbacks, squeezing past wide, slow-moving logging trucks, I began to love and to fear this man.

We smashed against a wall of mountains and drove through it, higher and higher up the Min River canyon, above a current that bobbed with logs. The country began to look like a Chinese scroll: steep limestone peaks covered with forest, cascades hurtling off cliffs. The houses changed. High on open slopes planted with corn and barley, they were now made of stone, flat-roofed, with bright lines of corn drying on the eaves and prayer flags flying off the corners.

We arrived in Maerkam long after nightfall. In this picturesque Tibetan town on the banks of the So Muo River, the government has built a handful of concrete monstrosities to house workers, soldiers, and visitors; the hospital looks the same, and the school. That night we didn't notice any of it. We lugged our bags to the top floor of the guest house, huffing with the altitude, and I wrinkled my nose at the stale meaty smell running through the chill corridors. A woman let us into our rooms—in China you are rarely issued your own key—and we fell into hard beds with heavy quilts. I dreamt about the river that we would run the next day.

Morning broke cold and drizzly. Groggy, we filed through a stadium-size dining hall where hundreds of Chinese clattered bowls beneath a huge mural of a panda drinking at a mountain lake, then went into our own private back room. Breakfast was peppered yak, sliced heart, rice gruel, and, thank God, hard-boiled eggs.

I remember bravely working through the dishes, and giving Fiona grief for being so damned British; she said that she and Dave had stayed up late drinking port and eating digestive biscuits. I teased Dave for not eating the yolks of his eggs. "You always used to," exclaimed Fiona. "before we were married." I took the hard little one-balls, put them on a platter, and cued up with a chopstick. *Bing.* A long corner shot sent a yolk across the table. Dave laughed, and Mark Wieprecht, a stocky architect from Oregon, said, "Maerkam Fats."

The rest of the day burns in my memory, though my journal entry is only one line. It was all I could bring myself to write.

We were excited. After so many weeks of preparation, of visa applications and passport renewals, plane flights and driving, we were at last going to get on the water. We'd warm up on the So Muo River before heading over to the Dadu. The So Muo is about the size of the Middle Fork of the Salmon, and runs right through town. We'd drive twenty miles upstream, then paddle it back.

Swift, milky water coursed through a narrow canyon beside the road. Ropes flying prayer flags were strung across the river, and logging cables swooped from the steep slopes. We saw no big drops in the water, and few eddies—just a continuous magic carpet of waves, with an occasional deep hole. Dave and Fiona sat in front of me, glued to the window of the bus, and I pointed out some river features. The couple were all ears, and a little nervous.

"This'll be great," I said. "It's mostly Class II and III. Shouldn't be any problem." My only concern, looking down at the rapids, was that there were no quiet pools—no places to rest and collect. But from what I could see, you'd have to try pretty hard to flip a boat.

We did pass one ledge extending halfway across the river with a very nasty hydraulic beneath it. Everybody saw it, remarked on it. But there was still half a river to maneuver around it.

At the put-in, our guides spread a cloth on the ground and cooked some noodles and tea. A Tibetan walking down the road in yakskin mukluks and a green wool greatcoat stopped to help us cut apart our taped paddles with his dagger, slicing off the tip of his finger in the process. He didn't even wince, smiling patiently while I rummaged around in the bus for tape and gauze.

By the time I was surfing a fast wave, waiting for the paddle rafts to organize, some fifty people had gathered on the bank. They came in logging trucks, farm trucks, army trucks, and Coaster buses; broad-cheeked women held babies, their long braids tied over colorful Tibetan headcloths. I twirled my paddle; Kim Reynolds, an Outward Bound instructor and ski-patroller from Aspen, stood her boat on end in a wave and raised a cheer.

Finally the two rafts shoved off, followed by me, Kim, and Scott in our kayaks. Our four guides had decided to join us. One had rafted with Warren on the Yangtze; two were mountaineering guides with no white-water experience; the fourth was our head guide, the humor-filled Mr. Lin, who had paddled a few times before, and was always up for anything. Kent Madin, codirector of Boojum and leader of the expedition, was running a fever, and had decided to stay in the bus to be healthy for the Dadu.

In combination with the chill, sunless air the water was finger-numbing cold and running faster than it had looked to be a couple of hours before. I know now that it was rising. Aside from that the river was pleasant. The rafts were moving well, their crews cheering as they passed. Dave Lyle, a Grand Canyon guide for more than ten years, captained one boat, and Mark Wieprecht, with twenty years of rafting experience in the Northwest, guided the other. The three of us in kayaks surfed, caught small shore eddies and sprinted ahead to catch the rafts.

Then the current picked up, the waves got violent, and as I came around a corner, all hell broke loose.

One of my favorite novels is *Sometimes a Great Notion* by Ken Kesey. It's about friends, logging, and the big, wet timber country of the Oregon coast. At the end, things fall apart. In a frenzied drive to skid the last logs into the river, Hank's friend Joe gets pinned under a log at water's edge. At first he's okay, because the water is only to his shoulders, and although he's in pain, he's tough. The two talk and joke. But the river is rising. Inexorably, it rises over Joe's head. That image, hard as a steel toe, has never left me.

It was with me on that bend in the So Muo. Just ahead on the left, I could see the line of the ledge we had noticed earlier. I paddled hard to the right, dropped around the ledge, and saw our fourteen-foot raft stuck beneath, riding the huge hole, empty, doing cartwheels.

A visceral knowledge, too complete and sudden for conscious articulation, can seize you. It's the heart-thump when the car hits an ice patch and slides towards a tree; you see the crash and can do nothing but cry out. I saw the tumbling raft, felt the shudder of tragedy, and thought, "Jesus, no—swimmers!"

Sprinting downstream, I saw a yellow helmet bobbing off the left bank. I flew toward it, pivoted and put my stern in the swimmer's face. "Grab the boat!" I yelled. "Grab the loop!" It was Liu, one of the Chinese mountaineers. I don't know if he was too panicked or didn't understand, but the current pulled him away before he could take hold of the kayak. In the same instant I saw a pile of logs just downstream, five feet from them a nearly submerged boulder, and stuck in the funnel between, a white helmet. Swiftly we were being sucked toward the jam. I stroked hard and hit the shore. "Swim!" I screamed to Liu. For God's sake swim. He didn't make it. His helmet joined the other.

Jumping out of the boat, I grabbed the throw rope and ran. I fell twice on the slick rocks, thinking nothing, thinking this is the way people die. Running beside me was Zhang, the Yangtze guide; I don't even know where he came from. We jumped onto the wet logs and clambered over them. All I could hear was tearing water and two men moaning. On the last log, each of us reached down, grasped the shoulders of

Liu's life vest, and pulled. Zhang was yelling, adding his cries to the terrible chorus: Liu was his old friend. "One, two, three, *heave*!" we screamed, and by some miracle, we yanked him free. Zhang's desperate yells were the only thing gluing my hands to the vest and we fell back, sliding Liu up onto the pile.

We dragged him over to a big log, where we laid him groaning, face down, then scrambled back to the other man. Kim and Scott were right behind us, followed by Mark, who had been guiding the flipped raft and, like Zhang, had somehow been flushed out of the hole and made it to shore.

We seized the man, two on the life vest, two on the arms. Water was surging around his neck and into his face. *Heave.* He didn't move an inch. Fingers gathered to grip again, and somebody, maybe me, yelled, "*Now!*" Nothing. He was wedged like a stopper in a seam of granite. It was then that I knew, somewhere beneath the rush and screams and gripping hands, that this man would die. Sucking air, catching breath, I caught Scott's eye: He knew it too.

"My right foot." Those words, barely audible, came from the man. Kim and I lay across the log, holding his life vest and helmet. By now, he was too weak to keep his head above the pummeling current. Scott and Mark rushed back to shore to make a snag line, a weighted bag tied in the center of a rope that they would toss over him, let sink, and pull back, in the hope of freeing a leg. Reaching down shoulder to shoulder, Kim and I glanced at each other.

"Who is it?" I yelled. I could barely glimpse his face.

"It's Dave."

"Dave?" There were three Daves.

"Of Dave and Fiona."

I guess I can say that my heart broke then. Stretched across the log, holding Dave's head, images flashed: Dave in Chengdu giving each of the women a speckled orchid; sharing a bag of peanuts with the table; reaching out at dinner to place a hand on Fiona's leg. Generous and warm, thirty-eight years old, on his honeymoon.

The snag weight skipped uselessly over the heavy current. It was just no good.

Dave didn't scream or even grimace. As he lay in the cold, rushing water, I could feel his patience. We were the experts. He had said as much days before when we'd each told our river experience. He and Fiona had been allowed to join the expedition because they were athletic and eager, and Kent figured it would be okay to have one inexperienced paddler per raft. With real respect and diffidence Dave had said, "I'm a novice. I'll be looking to you all to teach me." That patience was a subtle gift to his rescuers: I trust you.

The river was rising and it became harder to keep the water out of Dave's face. He drifted off, into shock. After an hour, the other raft came across the river. They had had a hard time getting Rebekah Bond, one of the five tossed paddlers, out of the water. She had injured her neck, and it took the rafters a long time to haul her up the steep slope to the road. Kent had jumped in Fiona's spot, and the raft arrived with pulleys, more ropes, and a dim feeling of hope.

We couldn't take the logs apart because they were all that allowed us to scramble out far enough to hold Dave up. Mark bravely stepped onto a jutting limb just below the funnel and got a line around Dave's waist. Dave Lamb quickly rigged a Z-drag—a rope with two opposed pulleys. The device could provide enough force to haul a fully submerged raft, but Dave didn't budge. They tried from upstream, downstream, the side.

Holding his head, trying vainly to keep water off it, I watched Dave go.

Death is simple. It surprised me, coming in clean and hushing everything. I wonder if there are hurricanes that really end abruptly in a whisperless silence. That's what Dave's death was like for me—at the end, it was a quiet relief.

With the help of twenty Tibetans who, seeing the commotion, had crossed a footbridge a mile downstream and run to meet us, we disassembled the logjam, placed Dave in the raft, and took him across the river.

Slowly, silently, we rolled back to town. Rebekah, racy Texan, lay flat across a seat, eyes glazed, neck damaged, and tried to wink. A heavy wave had knocked her out of the raft just above the ledge, and in the effort to get her back in, they had missed the move around the ledge and flipped. A freak accident.

The hospital was four stories of dimly lit concrete beside the river. A pig wandered in the shadows of the courtyard. Doctors babbled. They wanted to help Becky down the bus steps and lay her on a cloth stretcher. Dave Lamb, barrel-chested rancher and EMT from South Dakota, said, "Forget it." He stood in the door with his arms crossed. "I'm a doctor," he said. "She's not going anywhere without a backboard." So we found a piece of an old door, duct-taped Becky onto it, and gently lowered her through the window.

Kent and I climbed into the dark truck with Dave. We took off his helmet and propped him against a tube. Then Fiona climbed in to say good-bye to her husband; her sobs whispered down. My own drove me into the street, and once again I felt the fierce helplessness of watching, holding, being able to do nothing.

Beneath a cold half-moon eight of us carried Dave to the back of the hospital. We followed a bobbing flashlight over broken cobbles and glass and weeds, around deep holes. We walked along a littered wall, and I thought that there was nothing in the world heavier than the dead. We scraped through the narrow door of a concrete outbuilding and I caught my breath: On the ground lay two stone slabs, beside each a plank box, one of fresh lumber, the other of weathered scraps.

A debate ensued. Tibetans are short. Dave wouldn't fit into the new coffin. Some said to bend his legs, others said to try the old coffin, as it was a little longer. We did that. We hoisted him into it, laid boards across the top, and turned out the light.

Nobody who was working on the logjam, holding Dave's head, slept that night. Again and again I woke, watched the shadow of the mountain, watched the moon through the cold window. I desperately wanted to hold my lover, to curl in her arms, to tell someone I loved how big and patient this man was, how hard we tried, how life goes so easily. I saw the shearing water, saw Dave, heard our yells.

Fiona badly wanted a service out by the river, so the next morning Kim and Scott went off in search of prayer flags, only to discover that you can't buy them in Maerkam. The two hiked to a monastery on a hill. Destroyed by the Chinese in the Cultural Revolution, the monastery was being rebuilt, each decorative cornice and pillar carved by hand. An old monk stepped over the wood chips and listened to Kim and Scott's story through the English-speaking boy who'd brought them. When the boy was finished, the monk looked carefully at Kim, then at Scott, and sent them down the hill to a stone house beside the river. It was his personal place of worship.

There, beneath a giant prayer wheel and a figure of Buddha, Kim and Scott brushed ink out on a long wooden prayer press, and rolled out yards of yellow and white gauze. The boy climbed onto a ridge and cut young trees for flagpoles.

Dave was cremated that evening.

The next morning, the sun came out. The green water of the So Muo, subsided now by eight or ten inches, riffled through playful-looking rapids. Nothing made sense.

We planted the flags in a fan on the bank. Beneath them we placed flowers, purple asters that had been growing along the road, and sticks of incense. We said the Lord's Prayer, stumbling a little because few of us were in practice, and I read the Chinese poem "When Will I Be Home?"

Then out of the silence, like Quakers, we each talked about Dave. Xie, one of our guides, spoke last. He was very shy, and looked at his shoes. In halting English he said, "David was very kind to me. He asked me, have I ever been to America? I said no. He asked me would I like to go there? I said yes, it is very beautiful. One day I would like to go there. He said I must come to visit him. Now David is dead." We joined hands and sang "Amazing Grace"; some of these people could really sing.

A third of the group, departed—one dead, one injured, one widowed, and Kent, who'd gone back with Fiona and Becky to Chengdu that morning. We had come to the other side of the earth to run rivers, had made weeks of preparations, had raided savings. Now we were a small knot of tourists, dazed by grief, blinking in the first sun of a spittle-strewn courtyard.

Chinese officials rescinded our rafting permit. Nobody blamed them; nobody much felt like getting back on the water, anyhow. Instead, the next day, we would assume another itinerary. We would drive higher into the mountains and up onto the eastern Tibetan grasslands, to places no foreigner had seen in recent years.

Emotion breeds emotion. Raw, needing a change of gears, we filed under the colorful drinking panda to our back room at the guest house for a dinner of yak meat, yak organs, and searing *ma* peppers. We started drinking. The waitress went back and forth with tall bottles of Tsingtao. At the next table our guides were feting those in town who'd helped us: a doctor from the hospital, her mother, and a Tibetan police officer wearing a green uniform with red star epaulets. I picked up a liter of beer and went over.

Xie immediately handed me a small china cup filled with *maotai*—Chinese aquavit, dragon juice, acetone. Then the police officer leaned forward and spoke. He was a beautiful man, broad-faced, slight, with kind, wide-set eyes and thick black hair. Xie translated. "He says he would like you to sing a song. Then we'll drink. Then he will sing you a song and we'll drink. It's Tibetan custom."

I blinked. The man smiled at me, expectant. I can't carry a tune in a bucket. The table was silent.

When I was very small, my father would pull out his guitar and sing me cowboy songs. I remembered one, called "I Ride an Old Paint." I took a deep breath and launched in, starting slow and soft, then picked up strength. The man clapped in time, nodding his appreciation. It surprised me. I guess my father's voice sang through me, because the song was on key and melodic. When I finished, the table cheered and all rose. The man pressed his hands together and bowed to me his thanks. Then he touched my glass and we polished off the *maotai*. A shuddering heat twisted my stomach. Holding his cup close to his chest, the officer turned it to show that it was empty. Then we all sat, the man touched his fingertips lightly to the table, looked at me and began to sing.

His voice was perhaps the most beautiful I have ever heard: high, clear, and strong. His hands swayed, his eyes half closed. I was transfixed. A lifting rise and fall, and he was done. I stood quickly, pressed my hands together, and bowed. We clanked, beamed, and polished off another cup.

The rest of our group brought over chairs and joined us. The revelry began. More acetone was uncorked. The Chinese stood and sang "Red River Valley" in their native tongue. We did it in English. The whole table tore into "Jingle Bells" and there was much laughter. Scott made a telephone out of his hand, kicked his voice box into low gear, and rocked out "Chantilly Lace." Kim, with a voice sweet as a gospel singer's, sang a sad ballad she had written. When the *maotai* was gone, we drank beer. The officer said he would like to give us a song wishing us good fortune and we fell silent. Birds do not soar higher or more naturally than did that song. He brought down the house. Then he looked at me and spoke to Xie.

"He says you remind him so much of his brother in the mountains whom he has not seen in a long time," said Xie. "Your face, your happiness." I looked at the man, who was near tears. He lifted our half-full beer glasses and poured from one into the other and back; we raised them and drank.

When we were finally ready to leave, the man hugged me tight, pressing his cheek against mine. He stood at one end of the long dark dining hall, and raised his arm good-bye. Unsteadily, I threaded the tables. Whenever I looked back, he was there, alone, stretching his arm higher. I raised mine. The last time I saw him was when I turned the corner to take the stairs.

I went to sleep euphoric, and woke up with the worst hangover I'd had in fifteen years.

Lao Win, road warrior, took us higher. I wanted to be home. In the backseat, groaning, I looked up once and saw Colorado—a high valley, a stream, spruce and pine, meadowed ridges. It was a blur. Three sod houses with a pool table out front, balls misshapen and wobbly, a group of men playing in slanting light. Yak stomach and green gelatinous thousand-year-old eggs in another cold guest house in Zoigê, Dodge City of Sichuan: one wide market street with grass at either end.

I woke the next morning to the Great Plains, 1830. Our dome tents were huddled next to the truck and bus on a vast expanse of unfenced prairie which climbed to the north and broke like waves against a soft, grassy range crested with bluffs and spires of limestone. Scattered over the grass were small herds of yak and the white canvas of nomad tents. A faint, tobacco-rich scent of burning dung blew through the air. Feeling better, I went alone under the dawning sky and washed in a cold stream.

After I had dressed, I noticed three horses approaching our tents. On two of the horses were men; on the third, a woman carrying a child. About a hundred feet off, they stopped. I walked over. I felt as shy as they.

She was stunning: high wind-burned cheeks, tousled hair in long black braids, silver earrings, a hide longcoat trimmed with snow leopard and belted at the waist. Like the men, she wore the coat on one shoulder only, the other long sleeve tucked into her belt. Around her neck hung a necklace of heavy stones—jade, turquoise, and something yellow. In the folds of her coat nested the child. The woman looked down at me with liquid black eyes, not impassive, but very still. I smiled and she smiled back. The men's eyes lit up. On their belts they carried long daggers. One wore a slouch felt hat like a cowboy's. He was younger and had a boom box tucked into his coat.

The men dismounted and squatted beside their horses. They looked from me to our tents, to the sixteen-foot silver geodesic dome we used as the big house. I squatted beside them, dug in my pocket, and pulled out a pair of binoculars; I held them to my eyes, then offered them. The older man swiveled the glasses over the country, took them away, looked again. He trained them on a tent and pulled his head back at the sudden proximity. Softly, rapidly he talked to his son, passed him the binoculars, and turned to me with a broad grin that lost his eyes in leathered wrinkles.

Tentatively, the man reached out and brushed his fingers over the hair on my forearm. Our eyes met, and he started to laugh. Suddenly I realized that these people had never seen a Westerner. Of course he thought I was funny. He was smooth skinned, like a Native American, with little body hair.

Half an hour later, the woman dismounted and stood next to her horse. Our group was showing cameras and Swiss Army knives to the men. Jay Zuckerman, an Arizona rafting guide, juggled for the mystified child. The men were delighted. Soon they had shed their heavy coats and were laughing and riding our two mountain bikes in circles around the camp and down the road.

It was hard to make sense of anything? Waking at night, eating our meals in the dome, the pain of what we had been through surfaced again and again. Whatever we talked of, straining for lightness and humor, we always came around to that day, those few hours. But the grasslands were storybook. They challenged our pain with living fantasy, with grandeur, laughter, and horsemen.

The next morning, Scott shook me awake. "Get up! Get up!" he hissed. We were camped outside a small, mud-walled village, by another stream. I heard the thudding of horses' hooves pounding the sod. I stuck my head through the tent opening and rubbed the fog out of my eyes.

Forty horsemen, each with a prayer spear held high, were riding into our camp. They loped past the tents in a flashing of leopard trim, gold teeth, daggers, and iron filigreed stirrups. "Mother of God," I whispered.

They reined in, restless, then let their horses walk around us as they peered at the strange dwellings. I shoved on my sneakers and hustled out. I smiled. Big grins. A curious warmth that I have never felt among any other people arced through the morning air. At a loss, we passed up our binoculars and cameras. The men didn't know what to do with them. We pantomimed, and each item was circulated from one horse to the next, lost for ten minutes at a time. Then a man would ride out of the group and pass the object down, always to the right owner.

The younger men wore their hair long and loose. Some wore tall cavalry boots and felt hats, others sneakers or yak leather. The horsemen broke into small groups. They glanced at Judy Clapp, tall and blonde. They approached the tents and, too proud to stare, let their eyes flit over them, or leaned down quickly to look at the sleeping bags inside. A few dismounted, and one hoisted Dave Lyle, who's six foot six, onto his horse for pictures. He touched Dave's beard and laughed.

I never saw or heard a signal. Scott said an older man with a shaved head simply wheeled his horse. The men gave us their last smiles and nods, and then the whole bunch whipped into a run and rode away, kicking up sod, spears like forty masts against the northern hills.

For another week we traveled in that country. To Lamasu, where they were rebuilding the monasteries to the sound of constant drums. Where one night in a smoky tent a couple of us ate yak stew and drank rancid yak-butter tea with some of the nomad builders; we watched as an old man smiled toothlessly, spat in my bowl, and polished it clean. Where one couldn't nap because knots of women and children would gingerly unzip the tent and stare at the pale visitor.

On to the forbidden hot springs of Jiangzhou, to the travertine cascades of Huanglong. I was exhausted, by buses, by grief, by the rush of fantastic scenes that unfolded almost minute by minute. All of it was a countermelody, sweet music that could not sweep away the theme. The memory of Dave, of his quiet laugh, walked with me everywhere. When would I be home? It was the poem I had read for him at his service by the river. Home now, the poem comes to me like a chorus, often, like the soothing sound of running water through an open window.

> When will I be home? I don't know.
> In the mountains, in the rainy night,
> The autumn lake is flooded.
> Someday we will be back together again.
> We will sit in the candlelight by the West window,
> And I will tell you how I remembered you
> Tonight on the stormy mountain.
>
> Li Shang Yin

CAPFULL CREEK

Today I am going fishing. It is mid-September in the Rocky Mountains. The creeks and rivers are all low, all showing their bones. Broken logs are propped like wrecks on exposed rocks. In the hollows, and along the bottoms, the cottonwood leaves spin with a dry murmur. Color has already touched a few of the higher aspen.

There is one stretch I return to day after day. The creek runs out of the West Elks, cuts a valley from slopes which rise quickly to spruce and aspen and sandstone rimrock. Where the slopes are more gentle, the dirt road drops from its purchase a hundred feet above the water and meanders in the sun beside the stream, and the buckbrush and scrub oak open into small meadows.

To get there, I turn off the county road at Bob Littlejohn's and the track drops between two pastures where several dozen packhorses wait for hay. It crosses a plank bridge over Iron Creek, bends around the cabin and sheds, and follows the tributary I like to fish. Bob used to be the police chief down in town, had a house on Third Street ("What a fool," he said. "It ain't worth it.") and moved back to the creek to raise his horses and guide hunting and fishing trips. A mile upstream I pull into a grove of tall spruce beside the river and park.

Right now, this is all I want to do: fish. And return to a house, a home. I surprise myself. In the past few years I have seen remotest China, Alaska, Costa Rica, Siberia, the Caucasus, the Pamir and Tien Shan mountains. And suddenly I want a home. Rambling, once a compulsion and hunger, has become a profession. I crave the familiar and the intimately known. I want to stand very, very still and see what happens.

There's about two hours of fishing light left in the day. In the deep shade of the spruce the air bites. I don't have waders. I wear shorts and sneakers, and

I'm getting goose bumps, so I hustle with rod and vest and run down the narrow path, holding the rod high like a cavalry sword to keep it from snagging in the brush. I am so eager I have to tell myself to slow down, or I'll spook everything in the first pool.

I'm using dry flies. There's a tendency among writers who fly fish to become reverent and metaphorical, even a little superior. I would be that way too, but I just got the rod last Christmas. My first time out, a friend of mine who also doesn't know much showed me a few knots, and I said, "What fly should I use?"

He looked at the horizon for a second and said, "I saw a mosquito this morning."

"Me, too."

"Try this one."

I caught a trout. Since then I have caught almost every fish on half a dozen streams with a single kind of fly. "Match the hatch" is something I like to say; they say it a lot in the tackle shop where I buy flies to replace the ones I shred in the rocks and trees behind me. But I picked my fly out of the box the way you would pick a couch for your living room—something expressive, but not garish. Something pretty. It's an eastern fly, and looks like nothing a Colorado trout probably ever imagined. I think they go for it in a spasm of incredulity.

Stepping quietly onto the stones by the water, I free the hook from the cork handle, dab some liquid silicone onto the hackles to keep it floating, blow on it more than necessary, which is a quiet "Go get 'em," and cast up into the glare of current feeding the pool. The air stirs downstream, cool, cleaned of smells from the woods. It smells of sage a little, and of cold stones. Across the creek and high up, the sun is balanced on the ridge. In a minute it will make a blazing fringe of the trees at the top, and then this bend will also be in shadow. The fly drifts into sight, light against the dark patina of the pool. I retrieve it, and cast again, lower, just where I can see it, beyond a sunken rock, and hardly does it touch when there is the small blip and splash and pale flash of a rise.

Maybe wanderlust is stronger than any effort to sate it. Earlier this summer it bit so hard I did something stupid. I bought a big motorcycle from my brother-in-law in New York City, and flew from Denver to get it. I had never driven a motorcycle more than ten blocks. It was black and shiny and low slung, 1100 cc's, and it took me half an hour to get the nerve up to drive it off the sidewalk into traffic. At an intersection in rural Pennsylvania I stopped at a light and didn't get my foot down fast enough and fell over at a standstill. There was a McDonald's across the street, with a wall of mirrored windows, and I imagined behind them a hundred shaking heads. I was about to eat lunch in that town; I drove thirty more miles before I had shed enough embarrassment to stop. Aside from that I did okay. I had no itinerary and I got a kick out of cruising some of the smaller highways I had never seen before.

Drifters love to tell you about freedom and adventure and speed and choice. There is nothing quite like coming to an intersection, say in the desert where the spaces are widest, and being beholden to no one. It's true. But this is not the whole truth, nor the essential one. The essence of continuous travel is solitude.

What drifters never tell you is that they too must shore themselves against the loneliness. They telephone their families. They miss their sweethearts, and return like kites to the hands of people who love them. As fast as they travel, obligations enmesh them: they pay taxes, liability insurance, and bail. And the fright which can accompany the joys of constant choice wears them down. Complete and solitary responsibility for oneself can become a burden, and they get tired of moving. After a while, they, like me, are willing to make a home.

I can tell by the tug and tremor that the fish is small. Still, I am excited. What I love most about fishing is how intense deliberateness breaks into the sudden ecstatic feel of two lives, connected. I pull the line in with my left hand, but it is the right, on the rod, which feels most the urgency and violent will of the little rainbow. I reach for my net, and as I raise the tip of the rod to bring him in the last ten feet, the fish breaks water, and half out of it, hauled in, struggles into the green mesh. I am talking to him all the time now, telling him to hold still, "Hold still, baby, *Hold still*! You're all right . . ." trying to get the hook free and talking and talking.

I have a friend, Gary, who spent fifteen years hitchhiking all over the country, picking up work wherever he could. He once told me he felt betrayed by Guthrie and Kerouac and Neal Cassady. He said he started out caught up in the romance of the road, but that after a while he got confused. He said that he'd be out on the highway and he couldn't decide where to go, back to the last truck stop or on to the next town. I guess the hardest decisions are the ones that matter least.

I begin to wonder about myself. I wonder if continuous travel is flight from the fear that I don't really know anything important.

Another thing I like about fishing is the concentration of place. The intense focus on a single spot, a single small stretch of river, a pool, a riffle, an entire evening falling on three or four bends. When life is constant movement, it is a joy to stand still, to embrace with rapt attention the arc covered by a sequence of casts.

And while completely focused on the ripple of current beside a rock, on the unfurling line and relinquishing drop and drift of the fly, other things become focused too. The pyramid of Haystack Mountain rising out of the V of the valley far upstream. The gravel bar covered with young, purple-stemmed willows, just losing their green to the cool nights; grasses, and stiff mullein; small white moths roving over a part of the bend still in sunlight. And at the edge of everything the dark spruce, impassive, holding back the steep slope and the tide of night that already washes their dim trunks. The whole sweep of the place where one stands becomes a part of that concentration, a circle of awareness which is perceived without intent. The place becomes a part of you in the same way that in traveling so many of the most meaningful experiences loop in from the side, unsought.

Right now, this is the only place I want to be. Crouched over smooth stones covered with a dusting of fine silt and splashed with water from the fish and the net, talking to a small trout. And finally twisting the hook from his mouth and holding him loosely upright in the water while his gills work and tail idles, until he abruptly recovers from shock and realizes that he is unhurt and wriggles free, the dark green shadow of his life lost quickly among the refracting light and colors of the stones.

Set Free in China was designed and set in Garamond by Kate Mueller/Chelsea Green Publishing Company. It was printed on an acidfree paper by Book Press.